SCHOLASTIC

AF644755

Mastering Science 4

Name ______________________________

Class ______________________________

Photo attributions and credits:

Speech Bubble: Amada44(http://commons.wikimedia.org/wiki/File:Speech_bubble.svg). p.7: The following images are from Wikimedia commons: Author: Treesftf at Flickr (User: MPF) (http://commons.wikimedia.org/wiki/File:Pinus_roxburghii_tree.jpg), Paul venter(http://commons.wikimedia.org/wiki/File:Pinrox00.jpg), Paul Evans from London, United Kingdom(http://commons.wikimedia.org/wiki/File:Cedrus_deodara_Manali_2.jpg), Moni Sertel from Deutschland(http://commons.wikimedia.org/wiki/File:Cedrus_deodara_mature_pollen_cones.jpg), Crusier(http://commons.wikimedia.org/wiki/File:Abies_alba_Beskid_%C5%BBywiecki_3.JPG), User:Stan Shebs(http://commons.wikimedia.org/wiki/File:Abies_bracteata_2.jpg), Author: P Smith (User:Strider52)(http://commons.wikimedia.org/wiki/File:Moss_on_a_dry_stone_wall.jpg), User: Olegivvit(http://commons.wikimedia.org/wiki/File:Fern-leaf-oliv.jpg), Umberto Salvagnin from Italy(http://commons.wikimedia.org/wiki/File:Green_Lichen.jpg). pp.8-9: The following images are from Wikimedia commons: Forest & Kim Starr(http://commons.wikimedia.org/wiki/File:Starr_050518-1620_Azadirachta_indica.jpg), J.M.Garg(http://commons.wikimedia.org/wiki/File:Neem_(Azadirachta_indica)_in_Hyderabad_W_IMG_7006.jpg), Forest & Kim Starr(http://commons.wikimedia.org/wiki/File:Starr_0305140025_Peltophorum_pterocarpum.jpg), Bình Giang(http://commons.wikimedia.org/wiki/File:Hoa_va_la_muong_la_lac.jpg), LRBurdak(http://commons.wikimedia.org/wiki/File:Pipal_tree.JPG), Pratheepps(http://commons.wikimedia.org/wiki/File:Pipul_leaf.JPG), Photographer: Anuj Kumar Pradhan [User: (Eloquence)](http://commons.wikimedia.org/wiki/File:Kalimpong_cacti.jpg), LRBurdak(http://commons.wikimedia.org/wiki/File:Capparis_decidua_tree1.JPG), Balaram Mahalder(http://commons.wikimedia.org/wiki/File:Date_palm_tree.jpg), Docku(http://commons.wikimedia.org/wiki/File:Pepper_tree_in_Kolli_Hills.JPG), Aruna at ml.wikipedia(http://commons.wikimedia.org/wiki/File:RubberCultivation.JPG), AxelBoldt at the English Wikipedia project.(http://commons.wikimedia.org/wiki/File:Rubber_tree_leaves.JPG), LIC Habeeb at ml. wikipedia(http://commons.wikimedia.org/wiki/File:Kannimara_teak.JPG), Biswarup Ganguly(http://commons.wikimedia.org/wiki/File:Tectona_grandis_-_Kolkata_2011-05-03_2600.JPG), User: H2OC(http://commons.wikimedia.org/wiki/File:CottonPlant.JPG), Hannes Grobe(http://commons.wikimedia.org/wiki/File:Sugar_cane_madeira_hg.jpg); Dvellakat at ml.wikipedia(http://commons.wikimedia.org/wiki/File:Paddy_cultivation.jpg), Kalai (http://commons.wikimedia.org/wiki/File:Coconut_trees.jpg), Yasagan(http://commons.wikimedia.org/wiki/File:Ramesh_P_(25).JPG). pp.10-11: The following images are from Wikimedia commons: User: Lamiot(http://commons.wikimedia.org/wiki/File:Mangroves1.JPG), Author: http://www.flickr.com/photos/calliope (User: Ahura21)(http://commons.wikimedia.org/wiki/File:Baby_mushrooms_.jpg), Henry Mühlpfordt (http://commons.wikimedia.org/wiki/File:Verschimmeltes_Brot_2008-12-07.JPG), Dmst (http://commons.wikimedia.org/wiki/File:Amanite_tue_Mouche.jpg), Stefano Zucchinali (Ste3986)(http://commons.wikimedia.org/wiki/File:Digested_fly.JPG), Noah Elhardt (http://commons.wikimedia.org/wiki/File:Sarracenia_oreophila_ne3.jpg), (nl:Klein kroos) Lemna minor(http://commons.wikimedia.org/wiki/File:Klein_kroos_Lemna_minor.jpg), Eurico Zimbres Zimbres(http://commons.wikimedia.org/wiki/File:Water_hyacinth-flower.jpg), Hamachidori(http://commons.wikimedia.org/wiki/File:Nelumbo_nucifera_Oga02.jpg). p.12: The following images are from Wikimedia commons: KENPEI(http://commons.wikimedia.org/wiki/File:Potamogeton_dentatus1.jpg). p.19: The following images are from Wikimedia commons: Vikram Gupchup(http://commons.wikimedia.org/wiki/File:Asian_Elephant_at_Corbett_National_Park4.jpg), Aruna at ml.wikipedia(http://commons.wikimedia.org/wiki/File:Earthworm.JPG). pp.20-21: The following images are from Wikimedia commons: Rchampagne(http://commons.wikimedia.org/wiki/File:Guppy_04.jpg), User: DustyDingo(http://commons.wikimedia.org/wiki/File:Frog_on_bough.jpg), Marek Szczepanek(http://commons.wikimedia.org/wiki/File:Natrix_natrix_(Marek_Szczepanek).jpg), J.M.Garg(http://commons.wikimedia.org/wiki/File:House_Sparrow_(Passer_domesticus)_Female_in_Kolkata_I_IMG_3787.jpg), Orlovic(http://commons.wikimedia.org/wiki/File:Pet_rabbit_(2).JPG), ABF(http://commons.wikimedia.org/wiki/File:Coccinellidae(abf).JPG), L. Shyamal(http://commons.wikimedia.org/wiki/File:Spider_room_talakaveri.jpg), User: Inkub0(http://commons.wikimedia.org/wiki/File:Snail.jpg). pp.22-26: The following images are from Wikimedia commons: Paul Shaffner, Iringa, Tanzania(http://commons.wikimedia.org/wiki/File:Starfish_02_(paulshaffner).jpg), Twilight Zone Expedition Team 2007, NOAA-OE.(http://cs.wikipedia.org/wiki/Soubor:Reef3859_-_Flickr_-_NOAA_Photo_Library.jpg), James K. Lindsey(http://commons.wikimedia.org/wiki/File:Lumbricus.terrestris.jpg) , Richard Ling (http://commons.wikimedia.org/wiki/File:Pseudobiceros_bedfordi.jpg); User: Brian Boru (http://commons.wikimedia.org/wiki/File:Reef0484.jpg); Ltshears(http://commons.wikimedia.org/wiki/File:Diamondback_Terrapin.jpg); Marina Campos Vinhal (http://commons.wikimedia.org/wiki/File:Yellow_crab.jpg); Daniel Ahlqvist (Green Yoshi)(http://commons.wikimedia.org/wiki/File:Helostoma_temminckii_in_aquarium.jpg); Hans Hillewaert(http://commons.wikimedia.org/wiki/File:Giraffa_camelopardalis_angolensis.jpg); Krish Dulal(http://commons.wikimedia.org/wiki/File:One_horned_Rhino.jpg); Altaipanther (http://commons.wikimedia.org/wiki/File:Axis_axis_Kanha_4kl.jpg); Monkey: Yann http://commons.wikimedia.org/wiki/ File:Rhesus_Macaque,_Red_Fort,_Agra.jpg, Diliff(http://commons.wikimedia.org/wiki/File:Koala_climbing_tree.jpg); Koshy Koshy (http://commons.wikimedia.org/wiki/File:Indian_(Collared%3F)_Scops_Owl.jpg); Nyanatusita(http://commons.wikimedia.org/wiki/File:Hipposideros_lankadiva_Kelaart%27s_leaf-nosed_bat_2.jpg); André Karwath aka Aka(http://commons.wikimedia.org/wiki/File:Equus_grevyi_(aka).jpg), Marshmallow(http://commons.wikimedia.org/wiki/File:Brown_bear.jpg); Jiří Humpolíček (http://commons.wikimedia.org/wiki/File:Bedug001.jpg); Joelmills at en.wikipedia (http://commons.wikimedia.org/wiki/File:Hookworms.JPG). P.28: These images are from Fables. The following image is from Wikimedia commons: Scott Beckner (http://commons.wikimedia.org/wiki/File:Golden_Retriever_with_tennis_ball.jpg). pp.30-31:The following images are from Wikimedia commons: Alan D. Wilson (http://commons.wikimedia.org/wiki/File:Polar_Bear_ANWR_1.jpg), User: Pierrepoitevin (http://commons.wikimedia.org/wiki/File:Dromadaire4478.jpg), Liné1 (http://commons.wikimedia.org/wiki/File:Raphus_cucullatus_01_by_Line1.JPG); Erik A. Drabløs http://commons.wikimedia.org/wiki/File:Thomsons-gazelle.jpg; M.arunprasad (http://commons.wikimedia.org/wiki/File:Chamaeleo_zeylanicus.jpg). p.49: The following images are from Wikimedia commons: FDB (User: Sorenolin)(http://commons.wikimedia.org/wiki/File:FDBs_madpyramide_1982.jpg). p.55: The following images are from Wikimedia commons: Bill Murray(http://commons.wikimedia.org/wiki/File:Working_cotton_gin.jpg). p.58: Theses images are from Fables, except the following which are from Wikimedia commons: Daplaza (http://commons.wikimedia.org/wiki/File:Filet_de_p%C3%AAche_DSC00630.JPG). p.73: The following images are from Wikimedia commons: Tim Green (http://commons.wikimedia.org/wiki/File:Five_Pebbles.jpg); Thamizhpparithi Maari(http://commons.wikimedia.org/wiki/File:A_depiction_of_Cut_woods.JPG); de:User:Tomihahndorf(http://commons.wikimedia.org/wiki/File:Iron_lamp.jpg); Laurel F from Seattle, WA(http://commons.wikimedia.org/wiki/File:Cup_of_tea,_Scotland.jpg); Darren Hester(http://commons.wikimedia.org/wiki/File:Ice_cubes_openphoto.jpg); Itineranttrader (http://commons.wikimedia.org/wiki/File:AvocadoOil.png); Tysto(http://commons.wikimedia.org/wiki/File:Glass-of-water.jpg); Agency of the United States Department of Agriculture(http://commons.wikimedia.org/wiki/File:Orange_juice_1_edit1.jpg); Wolfgang Beyer(http://commons.wikimedia.org/wiki/File:Stromboli_Eruption.jpg); Love Krittaya(http://commons.wikimedia.org/wiki/File:Toy_balloons_9.jpg); Stefan Kühn(http://commons.wikimedia.org/wiki/File:Milk_glass.jpg); pic_p_ter(http://commons.wikimedia.org/wiki/File:Glass_cola.jpg). p.95: : The following images are from Wikimedia commons: SOHO EIT 284 Latest Image,url=http://sohowww.nascom.nasa.gov/data/realtime/eit_284/512/ Author SOHO is a project of international cooperation between ESA and NASA(http://commons.wikimedia.org/wiki/File:SOHO_EIT_284.jpg)

This edition specially created for Scholastic India.

First edition 2012
Reprinted 2012, 2013, 2014 (twice), 2015 (twice), 2016, 2020, 2021, 2022, 2023, 2024, 2025

ISBN 978-81-8477-928-8

Contents

 ISBN 978-81-8477-928-8

Introduction

Mastering Science is an exciting science series for levels 1 to 8. The books have been designed to fulfill the requirements of the National Curriculum Framework (NCF), which has been adopted by CBSE, ICSE and major State Educational Boards.

The series adopts a learner-centred approach, encouraging students to make connections between their role in their immediate environment and the world around them. The coursebooks are filled with lots of colourful photographs and illustrations that expose students to real-life everyday experiences from around the world.

In addition, the series prepares students to meet the challenges of the future by

- following pyramidal pedagogy
- encouraging exploration and innovation
- facilitating observation and logical analysis to support conclusions
- promoting independent learning

Learn More provides activities that hone the students' ability to absorb, infer, classify, experiment and predict.

Explore encourages students to analyse and question.

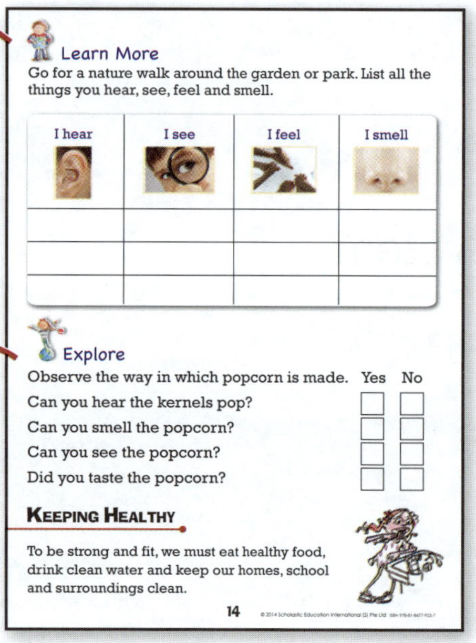

Learn More

Go for a nature walk around the garden or park. List all the things you hear, see, feel and smell.

I hear	I see	I feel	I smell

Explore

Observe the way in which popcorn is made.

	Yes	No
Can you hear the kernels pop?		
Can you smell the popcorn?		
Can you see the popcorn?		
Did you taste the popcorn?		

KEEPING HEALTHY

To be strong and fit, we must eat healthy food, drink clean water and keep our homes, school and surroundings clean.

14

I Care provides value education in levels 1 to 3.

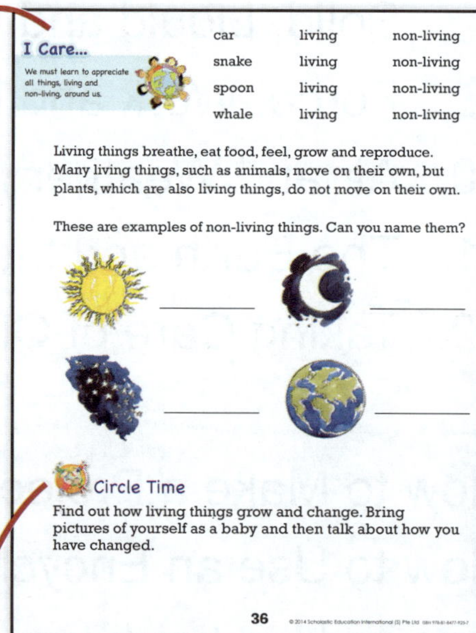

I Care...

We must learn to appreciate all things, living and non-living, around us.

car	living	non-living
snake	living	non-living
spoon	living	non-living
whale	living	non-living

Living things breathe, eat food, feel, grow and reproduce. Many living things, such as animals, move on their own, but plants, which are also living things, do not move on their own.

These are examples of non-living things. Can you name them?

Circle Time

Find out how living things grow and change. Bring pictures of yourself as a baby and then talk about how you have changed.

36

Circle Time promotes exchange of ideas and techniques while laying emphasis on working as a team.

 ISBN 978-81-8477-928-8

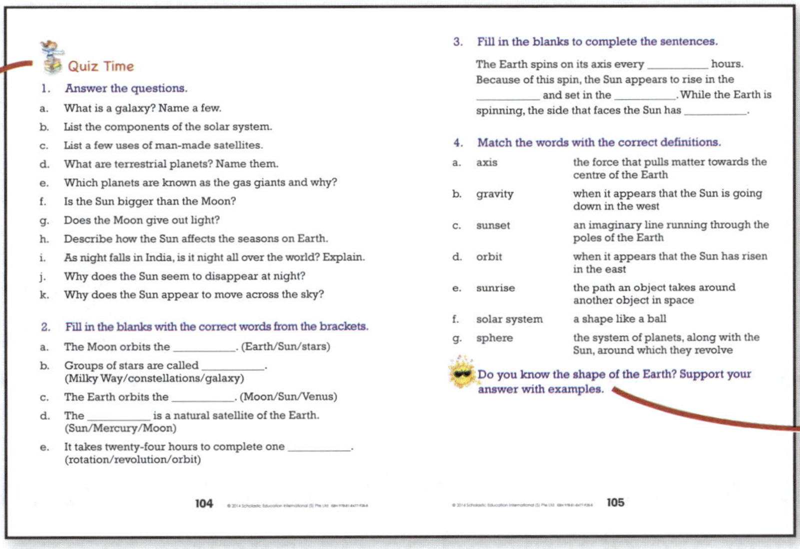

Quiz Time

1. Answer the questions.
a. What is a galaxy? Name a few.
b. List the components of the solar system.
c. List a few uses of man-made satellites.
d. What are terrestrial planets? Name them.
e. Which planets are known as the gas giants and why?
f. Is the Sun bigger than the Moon?
g. Does the Moon give out light?
h. Describe how the Sun affects the seasons on Earth.
i. As night falls in India, is it night all over the world? Explain.
j. Why does the Sun seem to disappear at night?
k. Why does the Sun appear to move across the sky?

2. Fill in the blanks with the correct words from the brackets.
a. The Moon orbits the __________. (Earth/Sun/stars)
b. Groups of stars are called __________. (Milky Way/constellations/galaxy)
c. The Earth orbits the __________. (Moon/Sun/Venus)
d. The __________ is a natural satellite of the Earth. (Sun/Mercury/Moon)
e. It takes twenty-four hours to complete one __________. (rotation/revolution/orbit)

104

3. Fill in the blanks to complete the sentences.

The Earth spins on its axis every __________ hours. Because of this spin, the Sun appears to rise in the __________ and set in the __________. While the Earth is spinning, the side that faces the Sun has __________.

4. Match the words with the correct definitions.

a.	axis	the force that pulls matter towards the centre of the Earth
b.	gravity	when it appears that the Sun is going down in the west
c.	sunset	an imaginary line running through the poles of the Earth
d.	orbit	when it appears that the Sun has risen in the east
e.	sunrise	the path an object takes around another object in space
f.	solar system	a shape like a ball
g.	sphere	the system of planets, along with the Sun, around which they revolve

Do you know the shape of the Earth? Support your answer with examples.

105

Quiz Time tests knowledge retention and serves as a quick recap of the lesson.

Higher Order Thinking Skills (**HOTS**) questions are included in levels 4 and above. These questions sharpen the students' skills of making inferences, understanding the logic behind a concept and thinking outside the box.

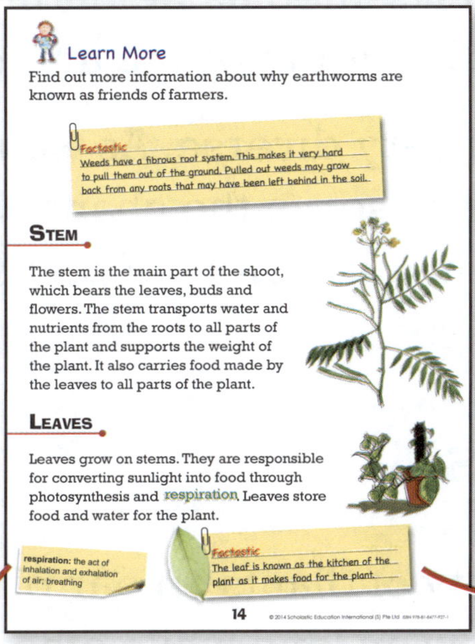

Learn More

Find out more information about why earthworms are known as friends of farmers.

Factastic
Weeds have a fibrous root system. This makes it very hard to pull them out of the ground. Pulled out weeds may grow back from any roots that may have been left behind in the soil.

STEM

The stem is the main part of the shoot, which bears the leaves, buds and flowers. The stem transports water and nutrients from the roots to all parts of the plant and supports the weight of the plant. It also carries food made by the leaves to all parts of the plant.

LEAVES

Leaves grow on stems. They are responsible for converting sunlight into food through photosynthesis and respiration. Leaves store food and water for the plant.

respiration: the act of inhalation and exhalation of air; breathing

Factastic
The leaf is known as the kitchen of the plant as it makes food for the plant.

14

New and difficult words are defined in the **glossary.**

Factastic imparts interesting information and facts related to the topic under discussion.

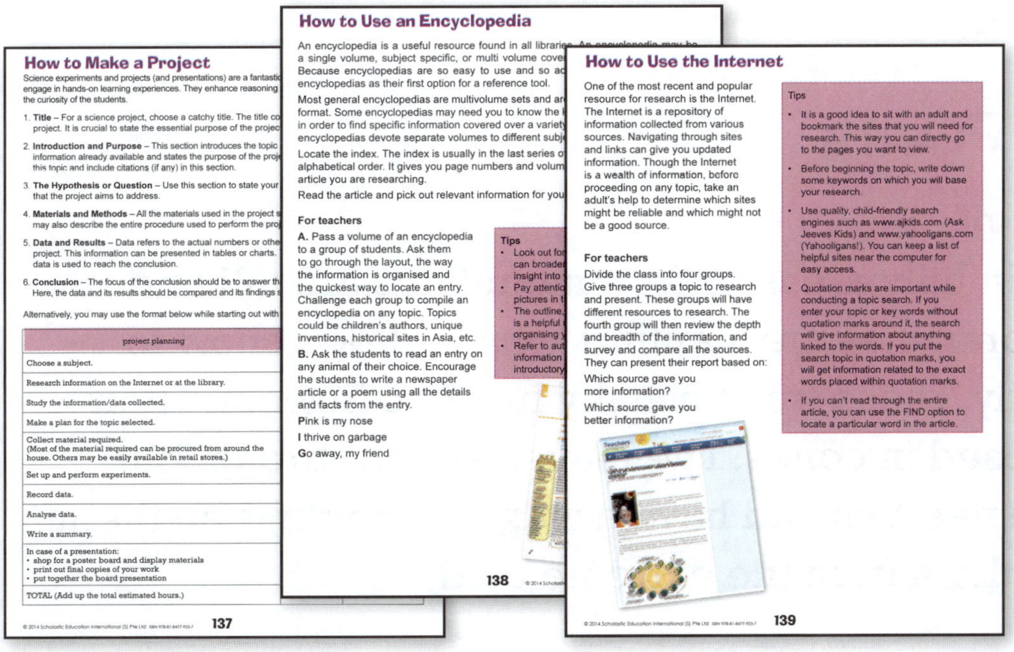

How to Make a Project

How to Use an Encyclopedia

How to Use the Internet

One of the most recent and popular resource for research is the Internet. The Internet is a repository of information collected from various sources. Navigating through sites and links can give you updated information. Though the Internet is a wealth of information, before proceeding on any topic, take an adult's help to determine which sites might be reliable and which might not be a good source.

137

138

139

Students are taught to use an atlas, the encyclopedia and the Internet in levels 3 to 5 to do basic research, individually and in groups, to present reports and projects. These help build the ability to learn independently.

 ISBN 978-81-8477-928-8

1
Plants

There is vast diversity among living forms found on Earth. All living beings are classified as belonging to one of the two kingdoms—the plant kingdom or the animal kingdom.

The plant kingdom is very diverse. As we move from one region to the next, we observe the changes in the weather, landscape as well as in the variety of plants and animals that are found.

Types of Plants

There is a large variety of plants on our planet. Some plants are terrestrial and grow on land while others are aquatic and grow underwater.

Terrestrial Plants

Plants on mountains

Trees growing in hilly areas and on mountains are tall and straight. Their branches are slanting, which allows snow to slide down easily. These trees usually have no flowers. Their seeds are enclosed in cones. The leaves are not broad, but are shaped like needles and have a wax-like coating on them, which protects them from the extreme cold.

 ISBN 978-81-8477-928-8

pine

deodar

fir

Ferns, moss and lichens are small sturdy plants that grow in the soil, on rocks or trees on mountains.

moss

lichen

fern

 ISBN 978-81-8477-928-8

Plants in plains

A large variety of plants and trees are found in the plains. These plants have branches that spread wide and have several leaves on them.

neem

gulmohar

peepal

Plants in deserts

Some plants and trees have adapted very well to the dry and harsh climatic conditions of the desert. As there is very little water available in deserts, the fleshy stems of these plants store water. The root system of these plants spreads over a large underground area in search of water. They have very few leaves, if any. A cactus has thorns instead of leaves, that help to cut down on water loss.

cactus

keekar

date palm

 ISBN 978-81-8477-928-8

Plants in areas with heavy rainfall

In areas that receive heavy rainfall, we see the growth of a number of trees and rainforests. A variety of plants ranging from tall trees, such as teak and rubber, and cash crops, such as rice and sugar cane, grow in these areas. Plants in these areas have many leaves and remain green throughout the year.

pepper

rubber

teak

cotton

sugar cane

rice

Plants in coastal areas

These plants survive in spite of the salty water and heavy rainfall along the coastline. Palm trees are common here. Coconut trees also grow abundantly in coastal areas.

coconut tree

 ISBN 978-81-8477-928-8

Plants in swampy areas

It is difficult for plants and trees to grow here as the soil in such areas is very sticky and salty. Mangroves have adapted to such conditions by growing breathing roots above the ground that help it to absorb air.

mangroves

Learn More

Use an encyclopedia to find out how the seeds of the coconut tree are dispersed.

AQUATIC PLANTS

Plants that live under or on water are known as aquatic plants.

There are three types of aquatic plants.

Floating plants

These plants have light and spongy stems, which enable them to float on water.

duckweed

water hyacinth

Fixed plants

These plants have thin, long and hollow stems that reach the surface of the water. Their roots are attached to the soil at the bottom of the waterbody. They have a waxy coating on the surface of their leaves to prevent them from decaying.

lotus

 ISBN 978-81-8477-928-8

Underwater plants

pond weed

These plants have thin and narrow leaves. The leaves absorb water, nutrients and dissolved gases directly from the water through their surface. Underwater plants do not have stomata to absorb these gases from air. Roots are often lacking and their only function is to anchor the plant to the ground.

Circle Time

Rohan covered a part of the garden with a wooden board. After a few days, he removed the board and observed that the patch of grass had turned yellow. Why did this happen?

PHOTOSYNTHESIS

Leaves are the food-making factories of green plants. They come in many different shapes and sizes. Leaves can be simple or compound. **Simple leaves** consist of a single leaf blade connected by a petiole to the stem. A **compound leaf** is made up of separate leaflets attached by a petiole to the stem.

simple leaf

compound leaf

types of leaves

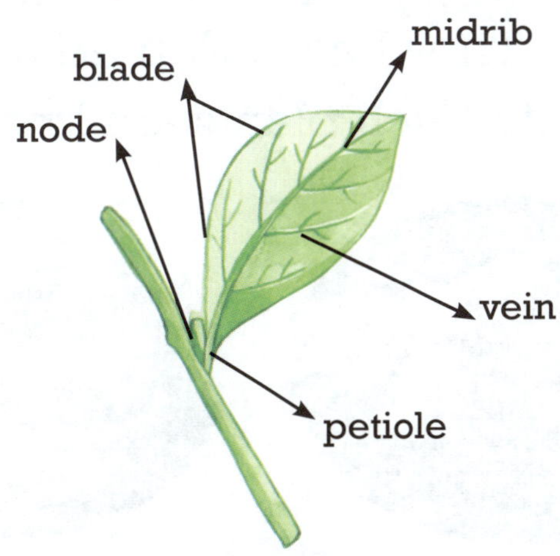

parts of a leaf

During the process of photosynthesis, leaves absorb light from the Sun. There are tiny holes on the surface of the leaves that allow air and water to go in and out of the leaves. These holes are known as **stomata**. Plants take in air rich in carbon dioxide through the stomata. The roots of a plant absorb water and nutrients from the soil and transport them to the stem. The stem then carries the water and nutrients to the leaves. The leaves use carbon dioxide and water to make glucose (sugar) in the presence of chlorophyll and sunlight. The extra glucose is stored in the form of starch and can be used later. Oxygen is produced during photosynthesis.

Non-green Plants

Mushrooms, toadstools and moulds are non-green plants as they do not have chlorophyll. Non-green plants cannot make their own food. They have adapted to absorb food and other nutrients from plants. Such plants are known as **parasitic plants**.

mushroom

mould

toadstool

 ISBN 978-81-8477-928-8

Some plants that cannot carry out the process of photosynthesis are **carnivorous** in nature. They have modified leaves to help trap insects and use the insects as food. The pitcher plant and the venus flytrap are examples of such plants.

venus flytrap

pitcher plant

Explore

Objective: To test the presence of starch in a green leaf using iodine solution.

Materials required: a green leaf, iodine solution, spirit and a dropper

Method: Take the leaf and boil it in spirit. Now, place it on a flat surface. With the help of a dropper, put a few drops of iodine on the leaf.

Observation: ______________________________________

Conclusion: ______________________________________

 ISBN 978-81-8477-928-8

Explore

Objective: To show that green plants need sunlight for photosynthesis.

Materials required: a green potted plant, spirit, iodine solution and a dropper

Method: Place the plant in a shaded part of the class for two or three days. Pluck a leaf from the plant. Boil the leaf in plain water and then in spirit. Rinse the leaf with cold water and place it on a flat surface. With the help of a dropper, put a few drops of iodine on the leaf.

Observation: ______________________________

Conclusion: ______________________________

Many factors affect photosynthesis.

- The more the sunlight available to a green plant, the faster the rate of photosynthesis.
- The more the amount of carbon dioxide in the air, the faster the rate of photosynthesis.
- The rate of photosynthesis is the highest in green plants at a temperature of 30°C.
- The lesser the amount of water, the slower the rate of photosynthesis. Without enough water, plants may lose their leaves or might even die!

 ISBN 978-81-8477-928-8

Carbon dioxide, water and sunlight are not the only elements that plants need to grow. Plants also require minerals. Soil contains minerals dissolved in water, which are absorbed through the roots.

Plants as Food

Factastic

Soil that is rich in minerals, known as fertile soil, is good for growing plants.

Most plants have a green substance in their leaves, known as chlorophyll, which gives them their colour. Chlorophyll allows plants to absorb sunlight and prepare food using carbon dioxide and water.

Animals depend on plants for their food, as they cannot manufacture their own food.

Humans also depend on plants for their food requirements. Many people eat meat as well, which is a good source of proteins.

Circle Time

Animals and plants are dependent on each other in many ways. Plants provide animals with oxygen, food and sometimes even shelter. Find out how plants are dependent on animals.

A **food chain** is defined as a series of living beings, each dependent on the next as a source of food. A food chain always starts with a **producer**, the living being that produces food. This is usually a green plant. All the other beings in a food chain are called **consumers**, that is, an animal that eats a plant or another animal.

 ISBN 978-81-8477-928-8

simple food chain

In this simple food chain, grass is the producer and the sheep and human are the consumers.

Quiz Time

1. **Answer the questions.**

a. Define photosynthesis.

b. Give two factors that affect photosynthesis.

c. What is a food chain? What role do producers and consumers play in a food chain?

d. What kind of plants grow in swampy areas? Why?

2. **Fill in the blanks with the correct words from the brackets.**

a. A cactus plant has _____________ to help cut down water loss. (leaves/thorns/flowers)

b. Trees growing on hills have leaves in the shape of _____________. (thorns/corns/needles)

 ISBN 978-81-8477-928-8

c. ____________ is produced during photosynthesis. (Oxygen/Carbon dioxide/Water)

d. The rate of photosynthesis is the highest in ____________ plants. (green/red/blue)

3. Fill in the blanks with the help of the words given below.

oxygen	carbon dioxide	photosynthesis	water
food-making	sunlight	chlorophyll	glucose

Leaves are the ________________ factories of green plants. Leaves contain a green substance called ________________. Leaves absorb ________________ from the air. Roots absorb ________________ and other nutrients from the soil. Chlorophyll converts water and carbon dioxide into ________________ in the presence of ________________. This process is called ________________. ________________ is produced as a by-product of photosynthesis.

4. A network of food chains is called a food web. Fill in the blanks in this food web.

a. Grass → _________ → lion

b. Grass → rabbit → _________ → lion

c. Grass → _________ → frog → _________ → kite

d. Grass → _________ → kite

 ISBN 978-81-8477-928-8

5. Indicate whether the following statements are true (T) or false (F). If false, write the correct statement in the space provided.

a. A cactus has thorns instead of fruits.

____

b. In a food chain, the Sun is called the producer.

____

c. Photosynthesis happens faster with more sunlight.

____

d. Photosynthesis gives us proteins and glucose.

____

e. Plants growing on hilly areas and mountains are tall and have straight branches.

____

f. Mangrove trees have breathing roots, which breathe underwater.

____

Will seeds germinate if you soak them in a liquid other than water?

 ISBN 978-81-8477-928-8

2
ANIMALS

Animals are living things that move, breathe and grow, but cannot make their own food. They depend on other plants and animals to produce food and energy. The animal kingdom includes mammals, birds, insects, amphibians, reptiles, fish and worms. Living things produce new individuals of their own kind by a natural process known as **reproduction**. They reproduce to sustain their species.

CLASSIFICATION BASED ON BODY PARTS

The animal kingdom, like the plant kingdom, is also very vast and diverse.

The animal kingdom is divided into two categories.

- **Vertebrates**: animals with a backbone
- **Invertebrates**: animals without a backbone

elephant

earthworm

 ISBN 978-81-8477-928-8

Vertebrates

Vertebrates are further divided into five groups.

group	examples	key features
Fish 	• Goldfish • Tuna • Cod	• Cold blooded • Have gills • Scales • Lay eggs in water
Amphibians 	• Frog • Newt • Salamander	• Cold blooded • Adults have lungs, larvae have gills • Moist skin • Lay jelly-coated eggs in water
Reptiles 	• Crocodile • Lizard • Snake	• Cold blooded • Have lungs • Dry scaly skin • Lay eggs with leathery shells
Birds 	• Pigeon • Sparrow • Ostrich	• Warm blooded • Have lungs • Feathers on body • Lay eggs with hard shells • Have wings
Mammals 	• Rabbit • Kangaroo • Human • Dolphin • Horse	• Warm blooded • Have lungs • Have body hair or fur • Give birth to young ones • Produce milk

 ISBN 978-81-8477-928-8

Factastic

Warm-blooded animals, such as mammals and birds, have a constant body temperature. Cold-blooded animals, such as reptiles, amphibians and fish, take on the temperature of their surroundings. They are hot when their environment is hot and cold when their environment is cold.

Invertebrates

Many small animals, insects and worms, spiders, scorpions, slugs and snails do not have a backbone. They do not have an internal skeleton made of bone. Invertebrates are divided into different categories.

group	examples	key features
Insects 	• Bee • Fly • Butterfly • Ladybird	• Six legs • Have three body parts—head, thorax and abdomen
Arachnids 	• Spider • Scorpion	• Eight legs • Have two body parts—head and abdomen
Molluscs 	• Snail • Oyster • Slug • Octopus	• Slimy bodies • May have one or two shells

 ISBN 978-81-8477-928-8

group	examples	key features
Echinoderms 	• Starfish • Sea cucumber • Sea urchin	• Symmetrical bodies • Usually have five arms
Porifera 	• Sea sponge	• Pores instead of mouth • Can exist in any shape
Annelids 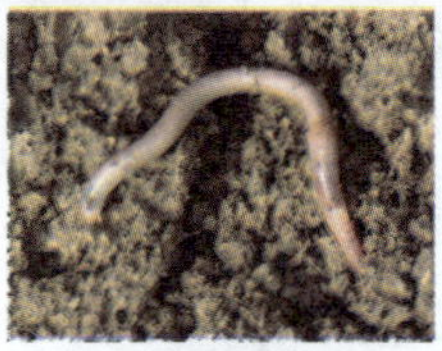	• Earthworm • Leech	• Segmented, tube-like bodies • Found in ponds or burrows in the soil
Platyhelminthes 	• Flatworm • Tapeworm	• Body not segmented and has head and tail ends • It has three layers of covering
Cnidaria 	• Jellyfish • Corals	• Two layers of skin covering the body • Between these layers is a jelly-like substance

Factastic

Arthropods have an exoskeleton (a hard outer coating) which protects their bodies. Human beings have skeletons inside the body known as the endoskeleton.

 ISBN 978-81-8477-928-8

CLASSIFICATION BASED ON HABITAT

It is easy to group animals according to where they live.

AQUATIC ANIMALS

An aquatic animal spends its entire life cycle in water. These animals can either be vertebrates or invertebrates. Most aquatic animals breathe through gills, but whales and dolphins breathe through lungs.

turtle

crab

fish

TERRESTRIAL ANIMALS

Terrestrial animals live on land and most of them breathe through lungs. These animals adapt themselves to the varied climatic conditions on land—the extreme cold of the mountains and polar regions, and the extreme heat in the deserts.

Factastic
'Terre' means Earth, so terrestrial means of the Earth.

giraffe

rhino

deer

monkey

 ISBN 978-81-8477-928-8

Animals in deserts have very light hair or fur on their bodies. Some animals in the deserts bury themselves in the sand during the day and become active only during the night.

Learn More

Use an encyclopedia to find out why giraffes have long necks.

Amphibians

Amphibians live in water as well as on land. Many amphibians begin life with gills and develop lungs over time. They are cold-blooded and regulate their body temperature according to the environment.

> **Factastic**
> Early amphibians were the first animals to leave the sea and move onto land. They formed an important link between fish and terrestrial reptiles.

Arboreal Animals

Arboreal animals spend most or all of their time on trees. These include the koala, lemur, flying squirrel, tree sloth, spider monkey, leopard, orangutan, chameleon, gecko, fruit bat, tree frog, snakes and lizards.

koala

Arboreal animals show a variety of adaptations. Tree sloths have huge claws that let them hang from trees without much effort.

Aerial Animals

Aerial animals are those that spend most of their time in air, typically in flight. Some animals, such as the flying squirrel and

 ISBN 978-81-8477-928-8

flying lizard, are able to glide through air for a short while. They may appear to be flying, but they do not have wings.

Aerial animals have hollow bones that make them light. Their bodies are aerodynamic in shape. While most birds can fly, the ostrich, penguin and emu are exceptions.

owl

eagle

bat

Classification Based on Eating Habits

zebra

A **herbivore** is an animal that eats only plants.

Animals that eat other animals are known as **carnivores**. They have very sharp teeth for tearing the flesh of their prey.

lion

Factastic
A predator is an animal that chases, attacks and eats other animals. The animal that gets eaten by the predator is known as its prey.

aerodynamic: the shape of a bird's body (similar to an airplane) that makes it easy for it to fly in air

 ISBN 978-81-8477-928-8

bear

An **omnivore** eats both plants and animals. Human beings, pigs and bears are omnivores.

Scavengers are birds, animals and insects that feed on dead or decaying matter.

vulture

Parasites live in or on other organisms. A parasite is dependent on its host for its life functions—to live, grow and multiply. It sucks blood and gets its nutrients from the host's body.

bedbug

roundworm

Factastic

Both humans and domestic animals can have hookworms in their bodies. Hookworms are common parasites that cause diseases as they suck out the nutrients from the host's body.

Learn More

A frugivorous animal is a fruit eater. Use an encyclopedia to find out more information on frugivorous animals.

 ISBN 978-81-8477-928-8

ANIMALS AND THEIR YOUNG ONES

ANIMALS THAT LAY EGGS

All birds reproduce by laying eggs. The parent sits on the eggs to keep them warm. The baby develops inside the egg. After a brief period of incubation, the egg hatches.

life cycle of a hen

Several animals, such as frogs, lizards, snakes and fish, also lay eggs to reproduce.

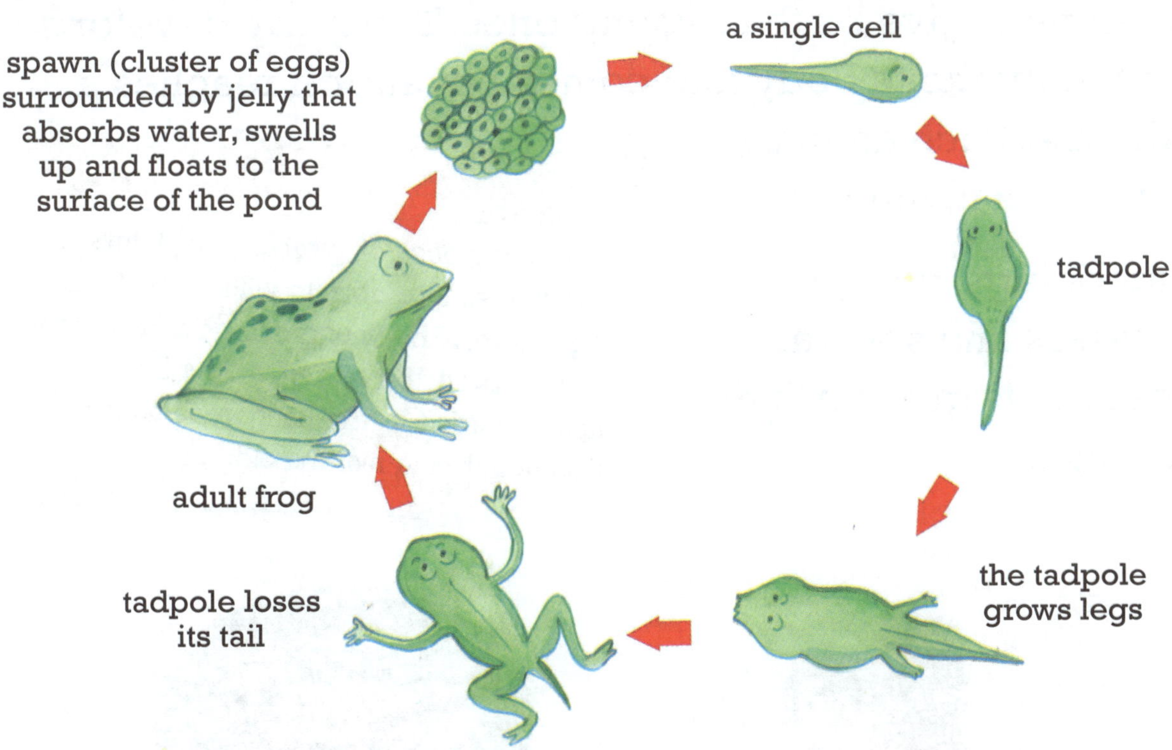

life cycle of a frog

incubation: the act of warming eggs in order to hatch them

 ISBN 978-81-8477-928-8

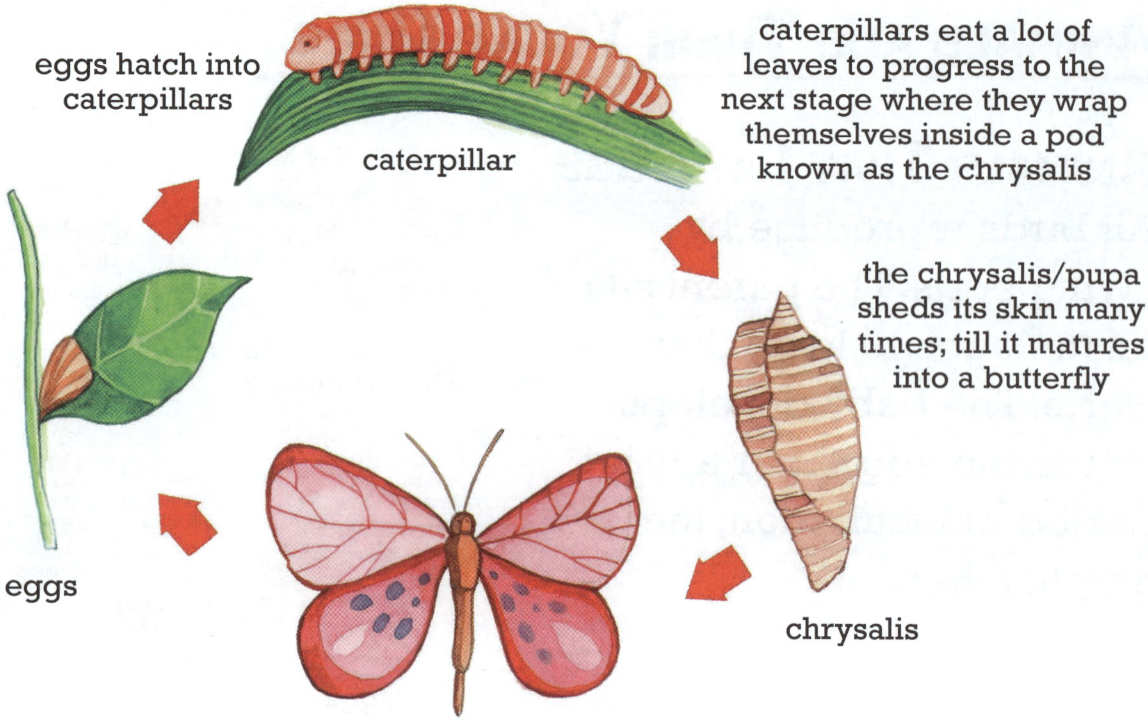

life cycle of a butterfly

Animals That Give Birth to Young Ones

Some animals give birth to young ones. The baby develops inside the mother's body and comes out after it reaches a certain size. Such animals are known as mammals.

Human beings, dogs, cats, lions, tigers and several other animals give birth to young ones.

Factastic

The young ones of giraffes, elephants and horses, are able to walk almost right away. The young one of a kangaroo, joey, is born the size of a lima bean and is nursed in the kangaroo's pouch till it is about nine months old.

 ISBN 978-81-8477-928-8

Learn More

Use an encyclopedia to find the names of five animals that lay eggs.

Mammals

The distinctive features of mammals are given below.

- Mammals give birth to babies.
- The young ones feed on their mother's milk.
- Mammals have hair on their bodies.
- They have well-developed brains.
- They breathe through their lungs.

Whales and dolphins are mammals that live in water.

Animal Adaptations

The natural home of a plant or an animal is known as its **habitat**. The natural conditions of that habitat, such as the temperature it experiences and the amount of rainfall it receives, are said to be the **environment** of that habitat.

All plants and animals have different features, known as **adaptations**, that they have developed over time. These adaptations allow them to survive and grow comfortably in their natural habitat.

Let's look at the following animals and see how they have adapted to their natural habitats.

Explore

Find out what adaptation by mimicry is.

 ISBN 978-81-8477-928-8

Polar bear

The polar bear lives in the cold regions of the world.

- It has thick, white fur to keep it warm. Its white colour helps it to hide in the snow when in danger.
- The skin of a polar bear is black in colour. This prevents the heat from escaping and helps keep it warm.
- It also has a thick layer of fat just below its skin to keep it warm.

Like the polar bear, there are other animals that enter a state of deep sleep in order to survive the cold winters when food is not readily available. This state is called **hibernation**.

Learn More

Use an encyclopedia to find information on animals that hibernate.

Camel

The camel is known as the ship of the desert. It lives in deserts which are very hot during the day and cold at night.

- Camels can survive for long periods without water. They can drink up to 46 litres of water in one go.
- Camels store fat in the hump, not water, which can be used for energy.
- They have flat, wide feet, which help them walk on sand without sinking.

 ISBN 978-81-8477-928-8

- Their nostrils have a narrow opening and their eyes are protected by two rows of thick eyelashes, which keep the sand away. Their thick hair protects them from the heat.

gazelle

Some animals, such as a gazelle, have very strong legs and are able to outrun their predators.

Some animals, such as chameleons, can easily blend in with their surroundings because of their body colouring.

chameleon

Extinct Animals

Like plants, animals also have different features which help them survive in their habitats.

Animals that are unable to adapt to changes in their surroundings slowly die out, that is, they become extinct.

Some people believe that the dinosaurs became extinct millions of years ago due to changes in the environment that they were unable to adapt to.

The dodo was a flightless bird, which became extinct due to human activities in the mid-seventeenth century.

dodo

extinct: no longer in existence; has ended or died out

 ISBN 978-81-8477-928-8

Circle Time

Observe some common birds. Which types of plants attract birds? Do certain bird species prefer to eat in a group or alone?

Quiz Time

1. **Answer the questions.**

a. Classify animals based on their eating habits.

b. Which features enable birds to fly?

c. What is the difference between warm-blooded and cold-blooded animals?

d. How does a camel survive the harsh desert climate?

e. What are invertebrates and vertebrates?

f. Name the different types of invertebrates and give two examples of each.

g. What are the key features of molluscs? How are they different from arachnids?

h. Name three types of vertebrates and give two examples of each.

i. How are amphibians different from fish?

2. **Fill in the blanks with the correct words from the brackets.**

a. Humans are ______________. (reptiles/invertebrates/vertebrates)

b. A polar bear's skin is ______________. (black/white/blue)

 ISBN 978-81-8477-928-8

c. Dolphins are _______________.
(amphibians/fish/mammals)

d. Terrestrial animals breathe through their _______________.
(skin/gills/lungs)

3. Animals adapt to their habitat in various ways. Write a few lines on adaptations of each of these animals.

a. camel b. polar bear c. tree sloth

4. Match the following.

a. parasites	eat other animals
b. arboreal animals	have dry scaly skin
c. scavengers	animals which have died out
d. carnivores	shape of birds which fly
e. aerodynamic	live on other living beings
f. reptiles	live mostly on trees
g. extinct animals	feed on dead matter

How is a dolphin different from a shark?

 ISBN 978-81-8477-928-8

3
The Human Body

The human body is a complex machine, made up of several important organs. These organs are a part of different systems in the body. Without these internal organs and systems, our body would be unable to function normally.

Skeletal System

The skeletal system provides shape and form to our body, supports and protects it, and allows easy body movement. Vital organs are protected by the bony skeleton—the brain is protected by the skull; the heart and lungs are protected by the rib cage.

Factastic

The adult human body is made up of a 100 trillion cells, 206 bones, more than 600 muscles and 22 internal organs.

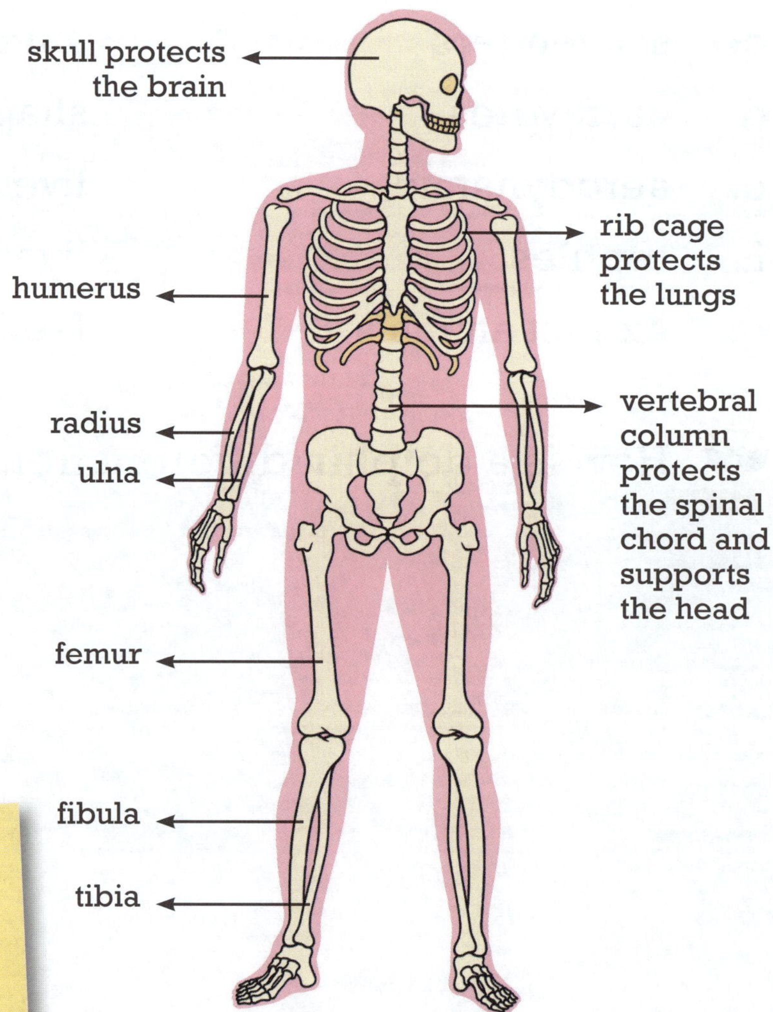

skeletal system

 ISBN 978-81-8477-928-8

Muscular System

Muscles are bundles of cells and fibres. They act as elastics that allow the bones to move and hence make movement possible. Muscles are connected to bones by tendons and bones are connected to each other by ligaments. Bones meet each other at joints. Muscles enable movement at the joints by contracting and relaxing. Some muscles in the body move on their own, that is, involuntarily, for example, the muscles of the diaphragm and the heart.

> **Factastic**
> There are 630 active muscles in the human body that work in groups.

Circulatory System

The **heart** is the most important organ in the human body. It is composed of muscles that pump blood throughout the body. It beats about seventy-two times every minute in an adult body. The heart pumps blood to the lungs where the carbon dioxide in the blood is eliminated and fresh oxygen is added to the blood. This oxygen-rich blood is then pumped to all parts of the body.

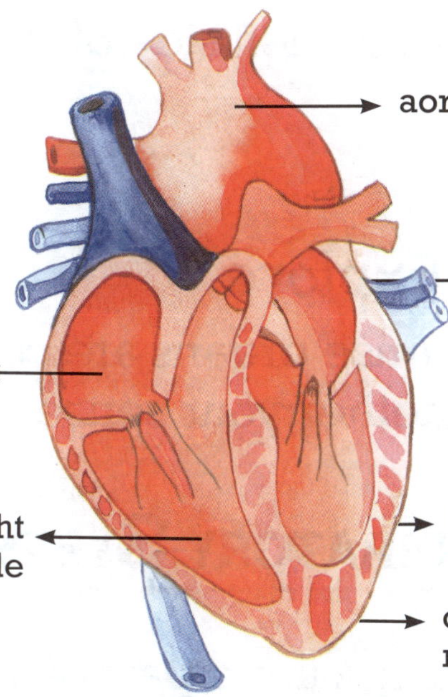

human heart

Learn More

Find out what a heart attack means.

tendon: a band of tough inelastic fibrous tissue that connects a muscle to a bone
ligament: a sheet or band of tough fibrous tissues that connects two bones or holds an organ in place
involuntarily: an action done without or against one's will

 ISBN 978-81-8477-928-8

Central Nervous System

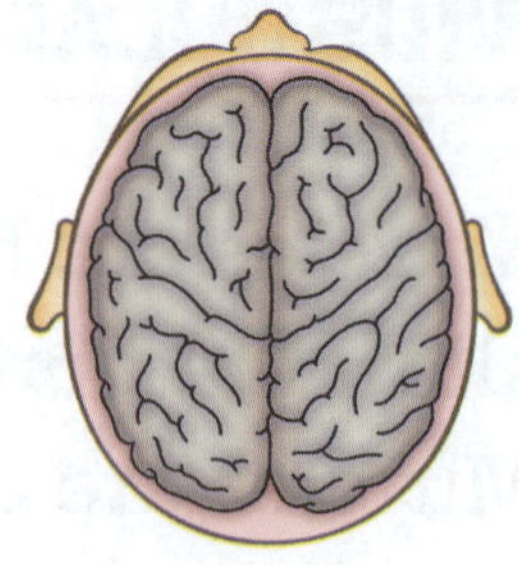

brain

The **brain** and **spinal cord** make up the central nervous system. The brain lies in the skull while the spinal cord is protected by the vertebrae. The human brain is the most developed compared to any other animal. It is the control centre for movement, sleep, hunger, thirst and all other activities important for survival. The human brain is divided into two parts. The left side of the brain controls the right side of the body, while the right side of the brain controls the left side of the body.

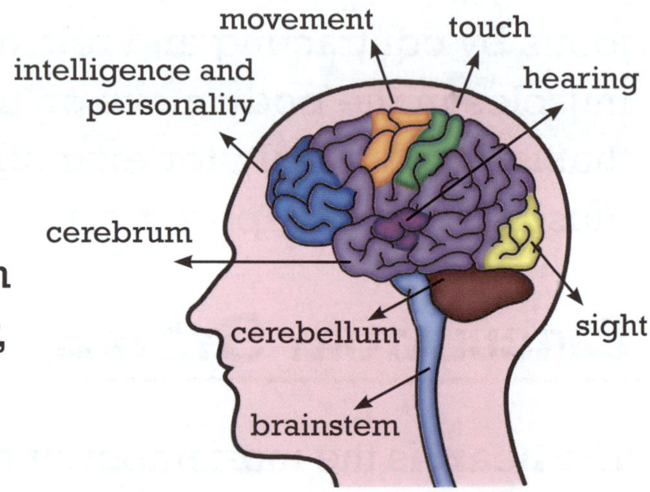

nervous system

Explore

Your sense organs are controlled by the nervous system. Find out whether your sense of smell alters your sense of taste?

Respiratory System

The **lungs** are a pair of sac-like respiratory organs that help us breathe. With each breath, the lungs add fresh oxygen to the blood, which is then carried to all the cells in the body; impure air is exhaled through the nostrils.

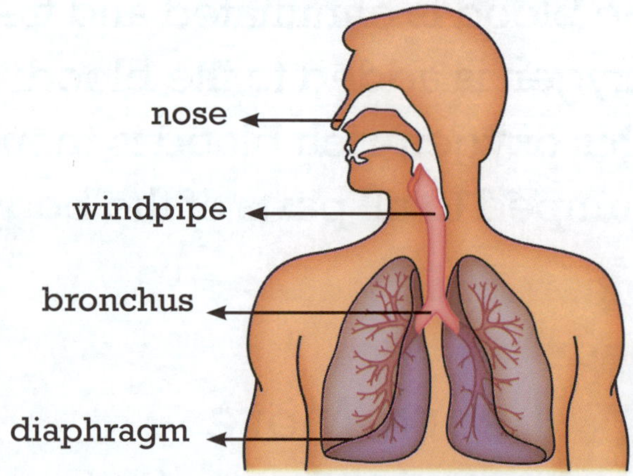

respiratory system

 ISBN 978-81-8477-928-8

Digestive System

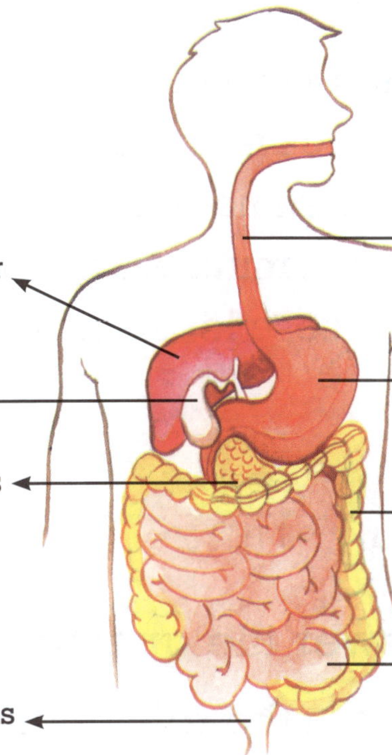

digestive system

The **stomach** is the organ of digestion. Shaped like a sac, it changes its size and shape according to the amount of food inside it. Food enters the stomach through the esophagus. The gastric juices break down the food in the stomach, before it is passed on to the intestine.

The intestines are divided into two sections—small intestine and large intestine. The small intestine is about 6 metres long. It is coiled up in the centre of the abdominal cavity. Most of the food is absorbed in the small intestine. The large intestine is wider than the small intestine, but is only 1.5 metres long. It absorbs water and is responsible for the excretion of solid waste material.

Excretory System

The **kidneys** are two small bean-shaped organs located at the back of the stomach. Their main function is to separate the toxins and other waste material from the blood and flush them out.

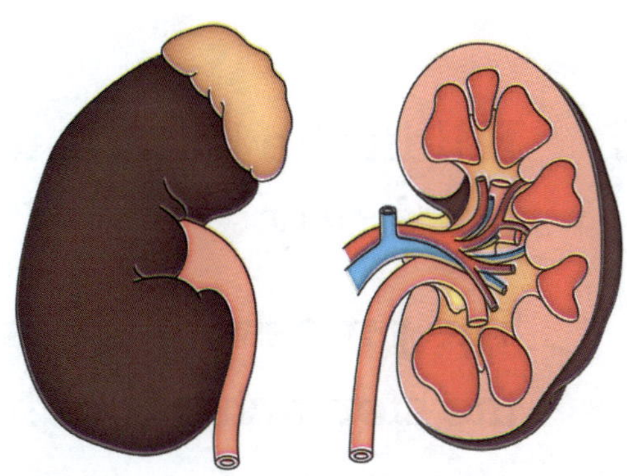
kidneys

 ISBN 978-81-8477-928-8

The **liver** is reddish-brown in colour and lies on the right side of the abdominal cavity. It helps to break down fats, filter harmful substances from the blood, store vitamins and minerals and maintain proper glucose levels in the blood.

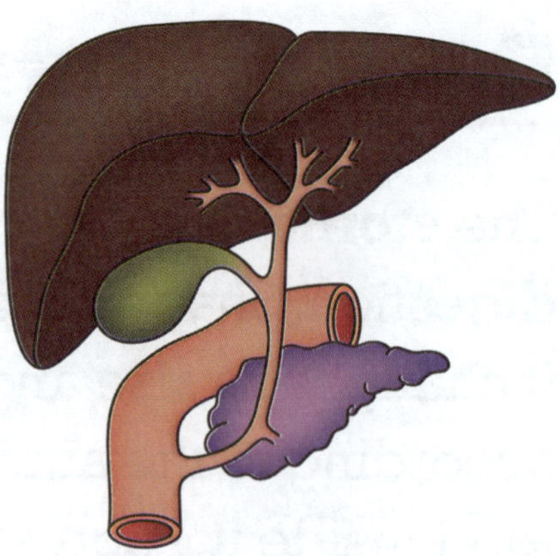

liver

Quiz Time

1. Answer the questions.

a. What is the role of the heart?

b. What is the difference between tendons and ligaments?

c. Give three functions of the liver.

d. Name the parts of the respiratory system.

e. What is a skeleton? What would happen if we had no bones?

f. How many bones are there in the human body?

g. What is the bone in our head called? What does it protect?

h. What do the ribs protect?

i. What function do the kidneys perform?

2. Fill in the blanks to explain the process of digestion in our body.

The process of digestion begins in the mouth. Food enters the stomach through the _______________. The _______________ _______________ mix with the food and _______________ it down. Food passes through the _______________ intestine,

 ISBN 978-81-8477-928-8

where the digested food is absorbed by the blood. The large intestine absorbs ______________ and finally waste material is passed out of the body.

3. Label the skeleton.

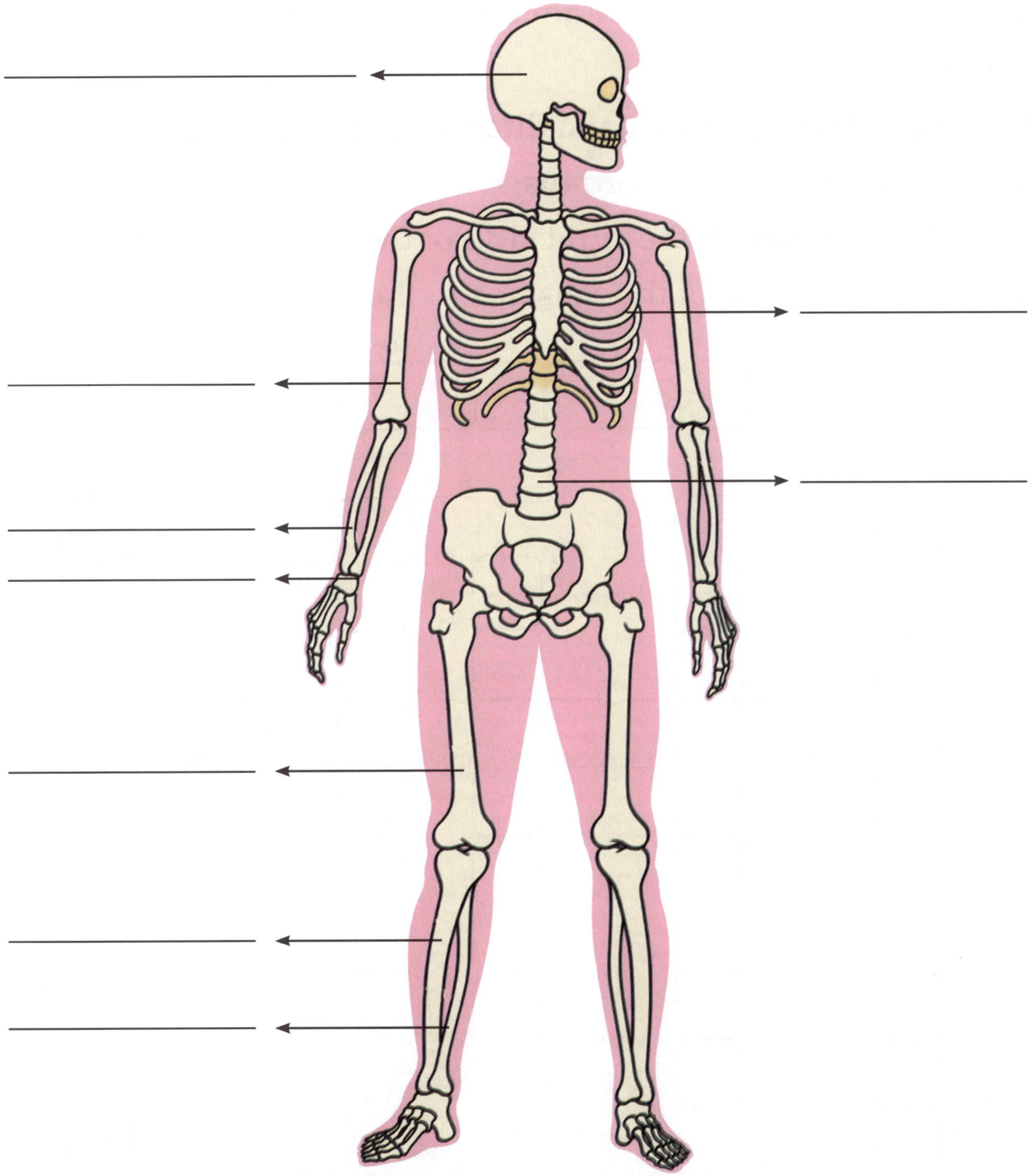

 ISBN 978-81-8477-928-8

4. Complete the crossword.

ACROSS

1. Bones are connected to each other by ________.
5. The main function of the kidneys is to separate the ________ and the waste material.
7. Muscles of the diaphragm and heart move ________.

DOWN

2. Food enters the stomach through the ________.
3. Lungs are ________ organs.
4. The liver lies on the right side of the ________ cavity.
6. ________ connect the muscles to the bones.

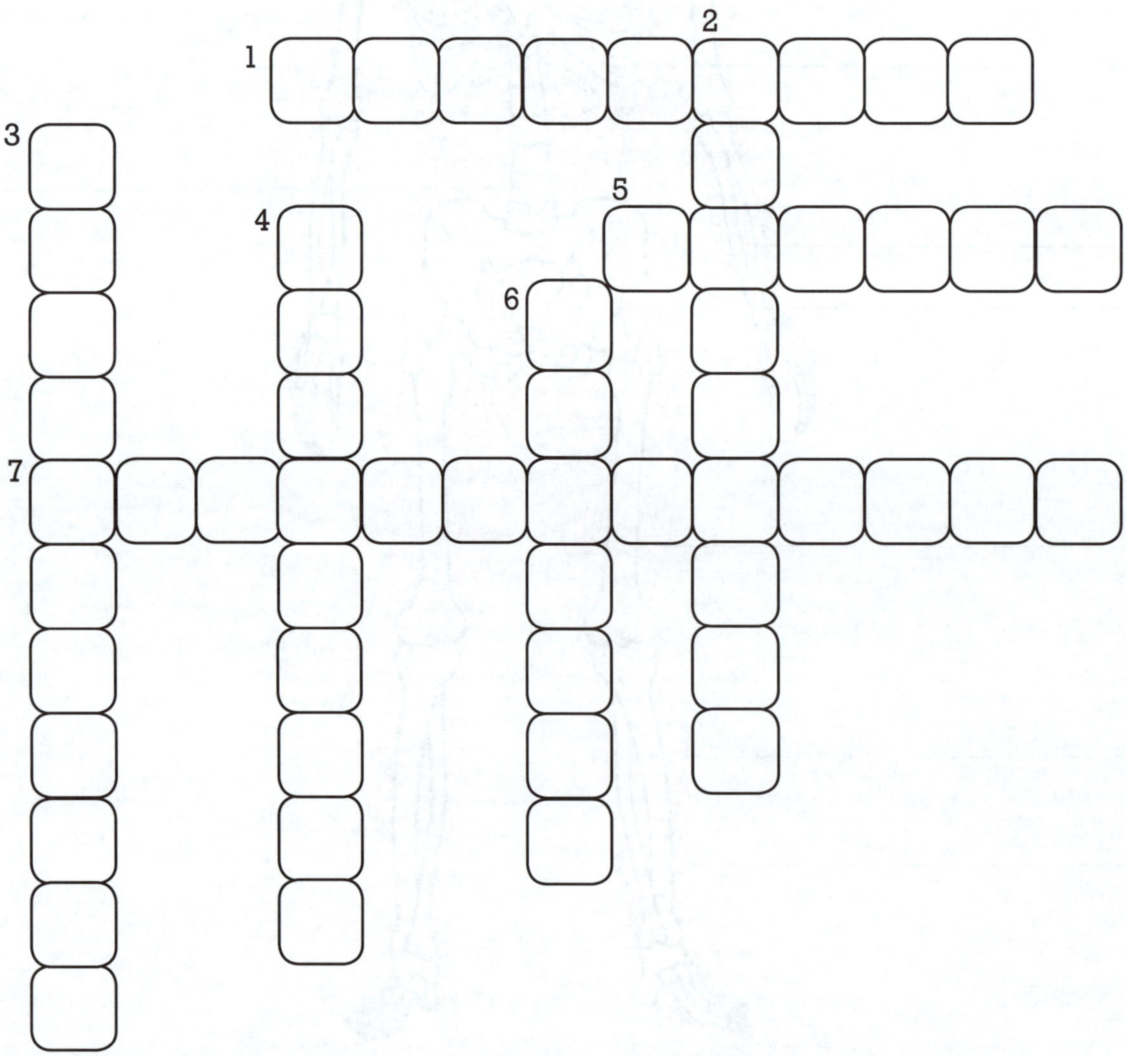

 ISBN 978-81-8477-928-8

5. Fill in the blanks with the correct words from the brackets.

a. There are ___________ bones in an adult human being. (210/206/260)

b. Tibia is a bone found in the ________. (skull/leg/face)

c. The largest part of the human brain is the ______________. (medulla oblongata/cerebellum/cerebrum)

d. The main function of the kidneys is to ____________________________________. (control the blood pressure/control the temperature of the body/remove waste from the body)

e. The lungs, nose and trachea are part of the ______________ system. (digestive/respiratory/muscular)

How do animals digest raw plant matter? Is their digestive system different from ours? Find out.

 ISBN 978-81-8477-928-8

4
Teeth

Most humans are omnivores and consume different types of food which need to be digested. The process of digestion starts with our teeth. Teeth are useful to us as they help us tear, cut and break up the food that we eat and make it easy to swallow.

Babies are born without teeth. The first set of teeth that a baby starts to grow at the age of six months is known as **baby** or **milk teeth**. Children have twenty teeth, but these start to fall out in a few years and are replaced by the much stronger permanent teeth.

An adult human develops a total of thirty-two permanent teeth. These start to grow when a child is about five or six years old.

> **Factastic**
> Chicks do not have teeth. They swallow their food whole. There are tiny stones in their gizzard that grind the food before it goes to the stomach.

Kinds of Teeth

There are four different types of teeth.

The **incisors** cut and bite. They are chisel or wedge-shaped to shovel the food inward. There are eight incisors in the front of the mouth—four on the upper jaw and four on the lower jaw.

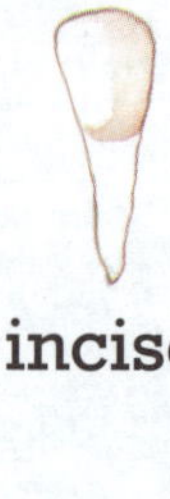

incisor

 ISBN 978-81-8477-928-8

canine

The **canines** are on either side of the incisors. They grasp and tear the food.

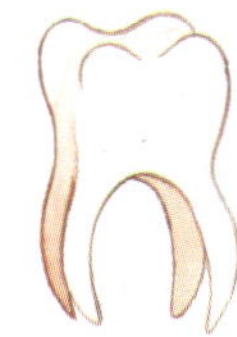

premolar

The **premolars** are located behind the canines. They have a flat surface, suitable for crushing food.

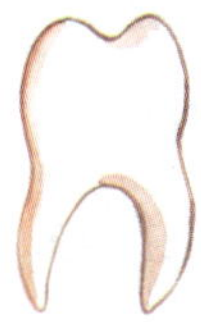

molar

The **molars** are the teeth at the back of the mouth. They are much bigger than premolars and have a flatter chewing surface. Their function is to chew and grind the food into smaller pieces.

> **Factastic**
> Plant-eating animals have very well-developed premolars and molars as they need to chew and grind their food a lot.

Anatomy of a Tooth

The tooth is fixed into the bony jaw socket and held in place by gums. The tooth is alive as it has a constant supply of blood and is connected by nerves to the central nervous system.

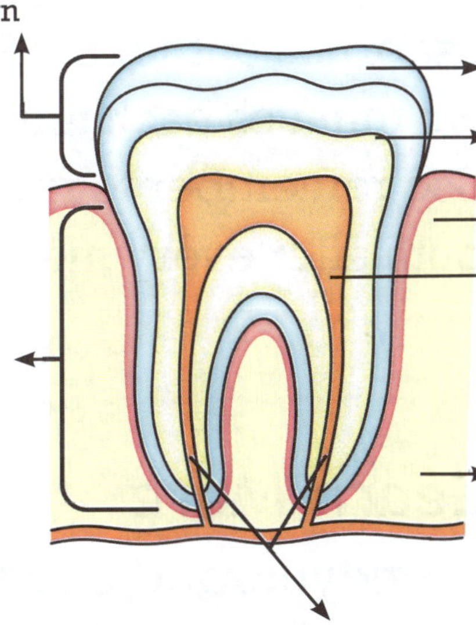

Each tooth has a **crown** and a **root**. The crown is the part that is visible while the root is inside the gums.

The hard, white part on the surface of a tooth is known as the **enamel**. It protects the tooth. Below the enamel is **dentin**, which is as hard as bone. Inside the dentin is the central chamber of the tooth. This part of the tooth is soft and is full of nerves and blood vessels. It is known as **pulp**.

 ISBN 978-81-8477-928-8

Tooth Care

It is very important to take proper care of our teeth. Sugary and sticky food items invite germs. As we eat, small bits of food get stuck in the spaces between our teeth. These small bits must be cleaned otherwise a yellow sticky film, known as **plaque**, develops. Plaque encourages germs that attack the teeth to flourish. These germs can damage our teeth and cause tooth decay. The only way to get rid of this plaque is to brush and floss our teeth properly.

We must brush our teeth twice a day—once in the morning before breakfast and once before we go to bed at night. We must brush our teeth for at least two minutes each time. We must also remember to rinse our mouth after every meal.

Learn More

Use an encyclopedia to find out more information on bacteria that cause tooth decay.

Teeth Problems

When teeth are not kept clean, **cavities** (small holes in the teeth) are formed as the teeth are attacked by germs or by the harmful microbes present in plaque. The germs present in plaque are very minute and not visible to the naked eye. We have to use a microscope to see them.

 ISBN 978-81-8477-928-8

There are different types of microbes.

Fungi

Fungi are usually the biggest type of microbes. Yeast is an example of fungi.

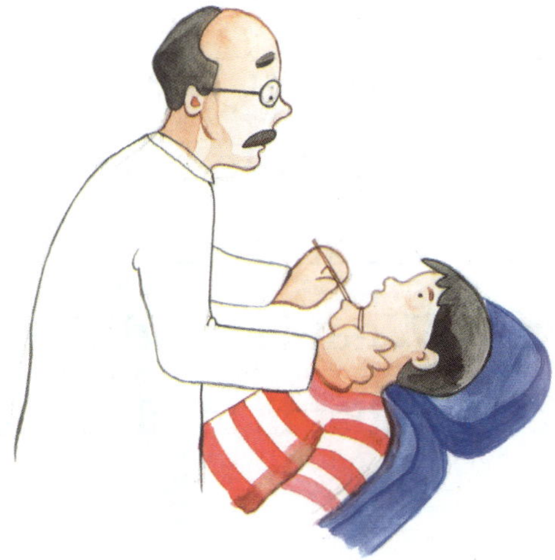

Bacteria

Bacteria are usually smaller than fungi. They can grow rapidly and may double almost every 10 minutes.

Viruses

Viruses are the smallest type of microbes.

When we have teeth problems, we need to visit a dentist.

Eating fresh fruits, vegetables and salads, protects our teeth from germs. As we need to chew this type of food, it improves blood flow to the gums.

Factastic

Teeth are primarily made of calcium. Calcium is very important for healthy and strong teeth. We mainly get calcium from milk and milk products such as paneer (cottage cheese) and cheese.

Explore

Plan a class visit to the dentist or invite a dentist to the class. Make a list of questions or queries that the students may have to ask the dentist about oral hygiene and dental care.

 ISBN 978-81-8477-928-8

Quiz Time

1. Answer the questions.

a. List three reasons for tooth decay.

b. What are molars? What is their function?

c. What is the difference between canines and premolars?

d. What is tooth decay? What causes it?

2. Answer in one word only.

a. Name the specialist who treats and takes care of teeth.

b. How many times a day should we brush our teeth?

c. How long should we brush our teeth for?

d. How many teeth does a newborn baby have?

e. What is the colour of the tooth enamel?

f. What holds the teeth to the gums?

3. Fill in the blanks with the correct words from the brackets.

a. Arun is four months old. How many teeth does he have? ____________ (three/four/none)

b. Sunaina is five years old. She has ____________ teeth. (no/temporary/permanent)

c. Akul is eight years old. He is likely to have ____________ teeth. (10/20/32)

d. Akul's mother is thirty years old. She'll have ____________ teeth. (20 temporary/32 permanent/20 milk)

 ISBN 978-81-8477-928-8

e. Ananaya is nine years old. Her teeth are ____________. (all temporary/some temporary and some permanent/ all permanent)

4. Match the following.

a.	acid	the outer coating of teeth
b.	milk teeth	doctor who looks after teeth
c.	gums	eats away teeth
d.	enamel	hold teeth in their place
e.	bacteria	hole
f.	cavity	germs
g.	dentist	temporary teeth

5. Make a list of all the food types that are good for our teeth. Also write the names of foods that encourage the growth of plaque and germs.

6. Indicate whether the following statements are true (T) or false (F).

a. We get a headache when teeth decay. ☐

b. Incisors are used for biting food. ☐

c. Bacteria cause tooth decay. ☐

d. Bacteria feed on the sugar stuck to the teeth. ☐

e. We must visit a dentist every twelve months. ☐

 ISBN 978-81-8477-928-8

7. **Fill in the blanks with the help of the words given below.**

incisors	hard	dissolve	swallow
molars	grind	cut	

We use our teeth for biting, tearing and chewing food. Our front teeth are called ______________. They ______________ the food into pieces. The teeth at the back of the mouth are known as ______________. They ______________ the food into smaller parts. This makes the food easier to ______________. Some foods do not require chewing, they simply ______________ in the mouth. Some ______________ and crisp foods require a lot of chewing.

8. **Mark the different types of teeth on the diagram.**

a. Incisors

b. Canines

c. Premolars

d. Molars

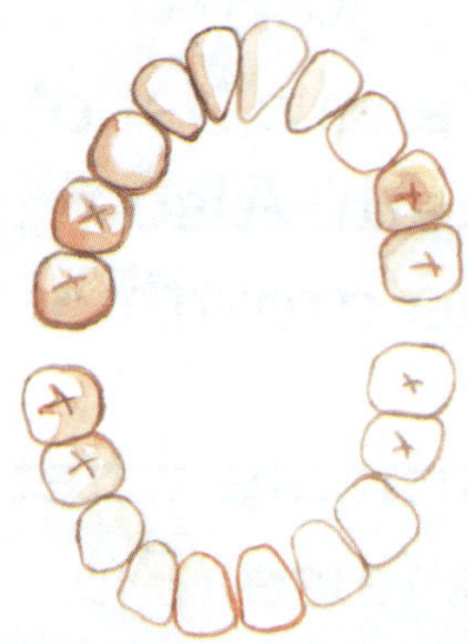

Have you ever wondered what the expression 'by the skin of your teeth' means? Find out.

 ISBN 978-81-8477-928-8

5 FOOD

We require a lot of energy to go about our daily routine. The food that we eat is converted into energy for the normal functioning of our body. To be in good health, we must eat food from all the food groups.

Healthy foods have a variety of nutrients that help us grow and remain strong. Each type of food helps our bodies in a particular way.

NUTRIENTS

The food pyramid represents all the components of a healthy, balanced diet and indicates the proportion in which they should be consumed. There are six different groups in a food pyramid.

- Carbohydrates
- Proteins
- Fats
- Minerals and vitamins
- Fibre or roughage
- Water

 ISBN 978-81-8477-928-8

nutrients	functions	sources
Carbohydrates	To provide energy	 Cereals, bread and potatoes
Proteins	For growth and repair of body tissues and to build muscles. They are also known as body-building foods	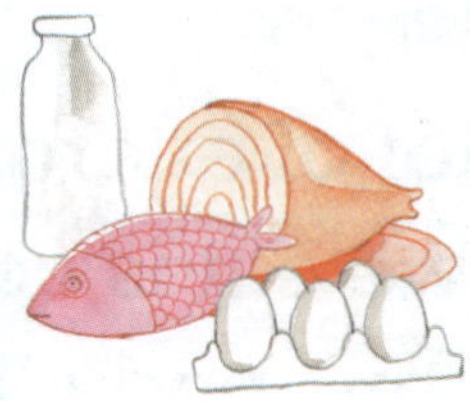 Fish, meat, eggs, cheese, dairy products, beans and pulses
Fats	To provide energy and heat. Also to store energy in the body and insulate it against the cold	 Butter, oil and nuts
Minerals and vitamins	Needed in small amounts to maintain health and protect us from diseases	 Salt, milk, fruits and vegetables
Fibre or roughage	Helps to ease the movement of food through the intestine	 Wheat, maize, jowar, ragi, oats, vegetables and fruits
Water	Needed for cells and body fluids, as well as for digestion	 Fruit juice, milk, water

 ISBN 978-81-8477-928-8

A **balanced diet** contains different nutrients in the correct amount to keep us healthy. Certain foods are not necessarily bad, but eating too much of them could be harmful for us. Junk food contains a lot of fat and sugar. We should avoid eating too much of it.

> **Factastic**
>
> The body also needs minerals, such as calcium, iron, potassium, iodine and salt, in small amounts. Calcium helps in the formation of bones and teeth, while iron helps in the formation of blood.

It is also important to drink plenty of water as part of a balanced diet.

Circle Time

Proteins are needed to build muscles, to grow and to repair tissues. Who needs to eat more proteins—children or adults?

Learn More

Find out five food items that are rich in calcium, iron and other minerals.

ISBN 978-81-8477-928-8

Food Preservation

Food preservation is the process of prevention of decay or spoilage of food so that it may be fit for consumption later.

Some foods, such as seasonal fruits and vegetables, are available in particular seasons and not in others. Hence, we preserve food so that it can be consumed at another time. There are a number of ways in which we can preserve food so that it may be consumed at another time.

Canning and Bottling

Making jams, pickles and sauces is a good way to preserve fruits and vegetables.

Drying

Fruits, such as grapes, apricots and plums, can be dried.

Refrigerating

We use refrigerators in our homes to store food items. The low temperature of a refrigerator prevents food from getting stale and from rotting.

Deep Freezing

If we freeze certain food items, we can preserve them for a long time.

Explore

Food preservation helps in many ways.

- Making seasonal food available throughout the year
- Decreasing wastage of food, as surplus food can be preserved
- Adding variety to the diet

 ISBN 978-81-8477-928-8

Quiz Time

1. Answer the questions.

a. What does the food pyramid represent?

b. Why do we need vitamins and minerals?

c. What are the minerals that our body needs?

d. Give two examples of carbohydrates.

e. Why is it essential for us to eat a healthy meal?

f. What constitutes a balanced meal?

g. What is food preservation?

h. What are the different methods of food preservation?

2. Rewrite the sentences correctly.

a. Proteins are energy-giving foods.

b. Carbohydrates give us more energy than the same amount of fats.

c. Eating cakes is a good way of getting roughage in your diet.

d. We preserve food so that it gets spoilt.

e. Carbohydrates are essential for stronger teeth and bones.

3. Write a short note.

a. Proteins

b. Fats

c. Fibre

d. Importance of food preservation

 ISBN 978-81-8477-928-8

4. Write down all the food items you ate yesterday. Indicate whether your food choices were healthy or unhealthy.

	food items	food group	healthy/unhealthy
breakfast			
snack			
lunch			
snack			
dinner			

Read the label on a jar of jam. Record the ingredients. What information do you get?

 ISBN 978-81-8477-928-8

6 CLOTHES

For thousands of years, humans have protected themselves from cold or hot weather by making clothes from fibres. There are two types of fibres—natural fibres, such as cotton, silk and wool, which are derived from plant and animal sources, and artificial or man-made fibres such as nylon and rayon.

NATURAL FIBRES

cotton gin

Cotton is a white, fleecy fibre that is obtained from the cotton plant. It grows around the cotton seeds. The fruit of the cotton plant is harvested and the cotton fibres are separated from the seeds in a factory. This is done using a machine called the **cotton gin**. The cotton gin was invented by Eli Whitney in 1793. The invention of the cotton gin industrialised the production of cotton fibre. The machine quickly and easily separates the cotton fibres from the seedpods, using a combination of a wire screen and small wire hooks to pull the cotton through the screen.

Small cotton gins were hand-powered while larger ones were yoked to horses or waterwheels.

 ISBN 978-81-8477-928-8

cotton bolls

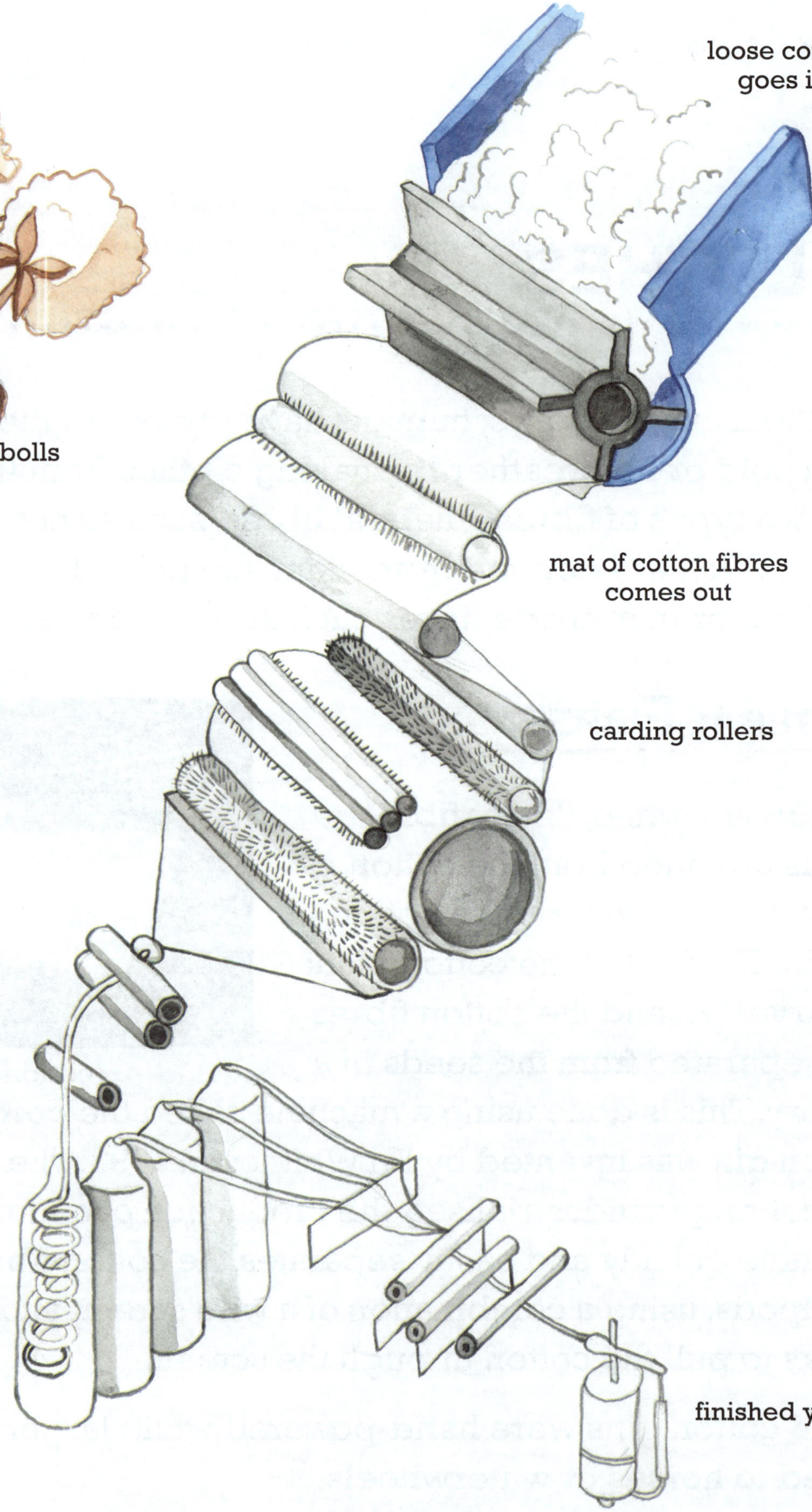

process of making cotton

 ISBN 978-81-8477-928-8

sheep are taken to be shorn

sheep have fleece shorn off

bales of fleece are taken to the mill

fleece is spun into woollen thread

woollen thread is woven into cloth

process of making wool

Wool is a soft, warm material obtained from the fleece of sheep. Wool fibres stretch easily and are good insulators. This is the reason we use woollen clothes to keep ourselves warm in winter.

 ISBN 978-81-8477-928-8

Silk comes from the silkworm. The silkworm caterpillar produces a liquid, which hardens into a thread when it comes in contact with air. The caterpillars use the threads to make cocoons to protect themselves while they change into moths. To make silk, the silkworm cocoons are dropped into boiling water. This kills the worms and loosens the silk thread, which can then be wound up. The threads can be woven into a smooth cloth called silk. Rearing silkworms for silk is known as sericulture.

Factastic

The hair of horses, camels and even pigs may be used to make fibres for paintbrushes.

Some other natural fibres derived from plants are flax and jute.

Synthetic Fibres

Rayon or artificial silk is made from cellulose, which is found in the wood of trees. The wood from trees is chopped into very tiny bits. It is then mixed with water and chemicals to dissolve the cellulose in the wood. This liquid is pumped through fine holes into another chemical solution, where it solidifies into fine threads. These threads can then be woven into fabric.

Synthetic fibres used in making parachutes, ropes and nets.

 ISBN 978-81-8477-928-8

Other artificial fibres, such as **terylene** and **nylon**, are made from chemicals. Terylene is used for cloth and curtains. Nylon is used for making parachutes, ropes and fishing lines.

Natural fibres are usually easy to dye. They need to be dipped into dye to colour them. Most artificial fibres are difficult to dye. Artificial fibres usually have colour added to them while they are being turned into thread.

Circle Time

How is our choice of clothing dependent on the weather? Give examples.

TAKING CARE OF CLOTHES

It is important to take care of clothes.

- Clothes must be washed well every day with a detergent to remove dirt and stains.
- Clothes can also be dry-cleaned. While dry-cleaning, petrol or benzene is used to remove dirt and stains.
- Woollen and silk clothes must be stored with mothballs and dried neem leaves. This keeps insects, especially silverfish, from attacking the clothes.

Learn More

What are vegetable dyes? Find out.

 ISBN 978-81-8477-928-8

Quiz Time

1. Answer the questions.

a. What are artificial fibres?

b. List the steps involved in the process of making woven silk.

c. How is rayon made?

d. What is nylon used for?

e. What are natural and artificial fibres?

f. Why do we need clothes?

g. How should we take care of our clothes?

h. Draw three items of clothing that can be made from wool.

2. Fill in the blanks with the correct words from the brackets.

a. Cotton is obtained from the ______________ of the cotton plant. (seed/fruit/flower)

b. Silk is obtained from ______________. (silkworms/butterflies/birds)

c. An example of a natural fibre is ______________. (nylon/jute/rayon)

d. ______________ leaves are used to protect clothes from insects. (Tulsi/Mango/Neem)

e. Fibres can be coloured using a ______________. (ink/dye/paint)

 ISBN 978-81-8477-928-8

3. Indicate whether the following statements are true (T) or false (F).

a. Cotton comes from the seeds of cotton plants. ☐

b. A silkworm produces silk to make a cocoon. ☐

c. Wool is the only fibre that comes from animals. ☐

d. Wool and cotton are natural fibres. ☐

e. Artificial fibres are difficult to dye. ☐

f. Nylon is made from chemicals. ☐

Read the labels of garments made of cotton, silk, wool and lycra. The washing and caring instructions for each are different. Why?

 ISBN 978-81-8477-928-8

7
SAFETY AND FIRST AID

Safety is of utmost importance to avoid accidents. Accidents can happen at home, at school or even in the park or playground. We need to be aware of things that can be dangerous.

However, sometimes, injuries and illnesses can happen even when we are very careful. It is important to take proper care at such times.

Learn More

Use a red pencil to underline the things that you should not do and a green pencil to underline the things that you should do.

1. Touch a plug.
2. Handle appliances in the kitchen.
3. Use knives and scissors under adult supervision.
4. If some water spills on the floor, you should wipe it.
5. Keep the bathroom floor wet.
6. Do not play with sharp objects such as blades or razors.
7. Cross the road only at the zebra crossing.
8. Run on the road.

 ISBN 978-81-8477-928-8

9. Never put your hand or any other body part out of a moving vehicle.

10. Walk up and down the stairs carefully.

11. Do not walk on the footpath.

12. Do not wear synthetic clothes while near a fire or firecrackers.

13. Play rough games in the park.

14. Do not push or hurt anybody in the playground.

15. Go swimming accompanied by an adult.

16. Consume medicines lying at home without asking anyone.

First Aid

When there is an accident or an injury, the first way to help is first aid.

First aid provides care to ill or injured people until medical help arrives. An important tool for first aid is a first aid box. A first aid box contains some necessary things that can help an injured or sick person until a doctor can see them.

The first aid box must be kept within easy reach. Gathering the necessary items in the box ahead of time can help handle an emergency quickly.

 ISBN 978-81-8477-928-8

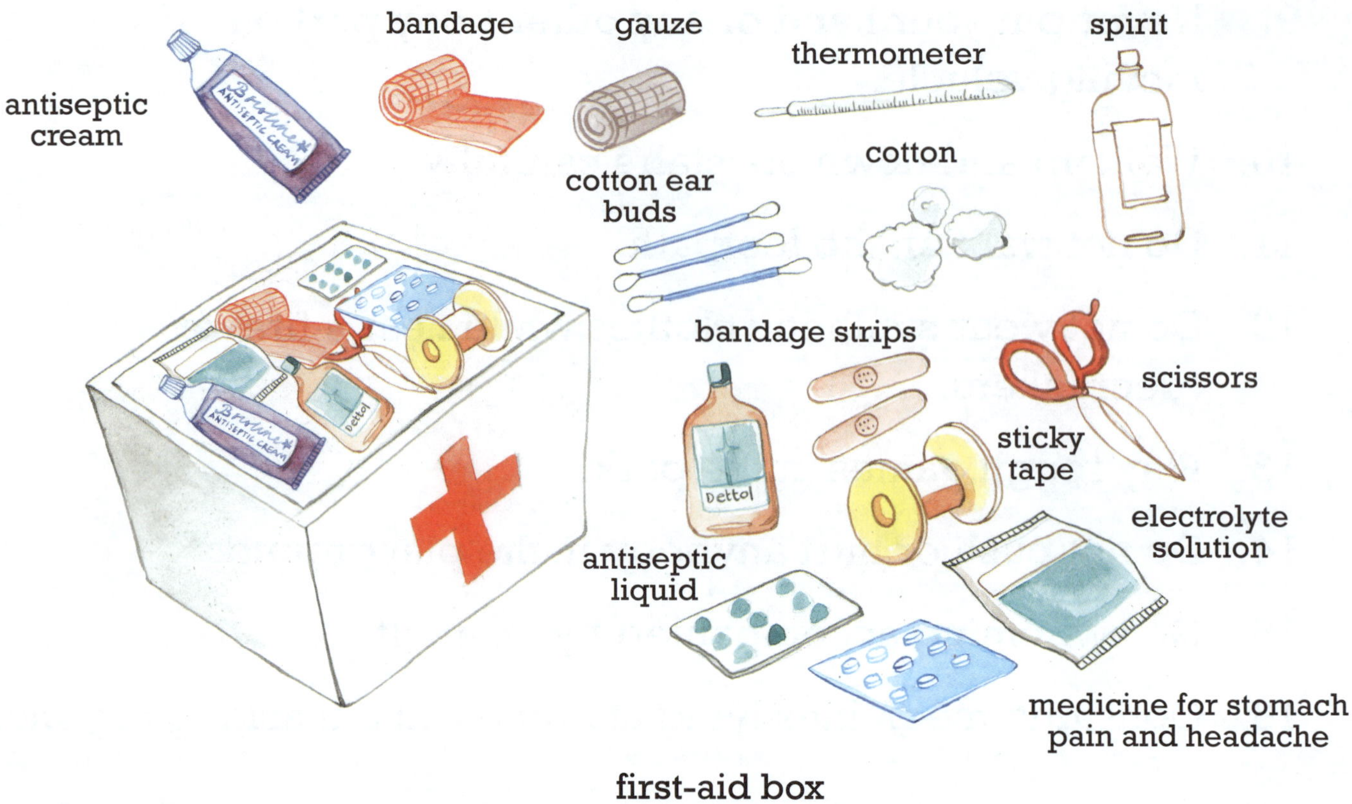

First Aid for Cuts and Wounds

- Wash the wound with clean water so that all the dirt is removed.
- Use cotton to apply some antiseptic liquid.
- If the wound is bleeding, then press lightly with a clean cloth or cotton till the bleeding stops.
- If the wound is not too deep, then dress it with a bandage.

First Aid for Burns

- Pour clean water over the affected area.
- Put an ice pack to stop the burning sensation.
- Apply an antiseptic cream on the affected area.

First Aid for Insect Bites

- Wash the affected area with soap and water.
- Put an ice pack on the affected area.
- Apply some calamine lotion on the insect bite.

 ISBN 978-81-8477-928-8

A few points to keep in mind in case a person gets hurt.

- Be calm and do not panic.
- Call an adult and a doctor immediately.
- Do not crowd around the injured person.
- Let the person relax.

Circle Time

List down the telephone numbers you think you might require during an emergency.

Quiz Time

1. Answer the questions.

a. What is first aid?

b. What should you do if you accidentally pour hot water on yourself?

c. Your sister is playing with a knife and gets hurt. What will you do?

d. List five safety measures.

e. Name the items that a first-aid box should contain.

f. Name one important thing to keep in mind when a person gets hurt.

g. What first aid would you provide if an insect bites a person?

 ISBN 978-81-8477-928-8

2. Fill in the blanks with the correct words from the brackets.

a. The first aid box should have a ____________. (speedometer/thermometer/water purifier)

b. You should not consume ____________ without a doctor's prescription. (biscuits/rice/medicines)

c. An ____________ cream can help heal the wound. (antiseptic/milk/chocolates)

d. We should never touch any appliance with ____________ hands. (bare/wet/dry)

e. When someone gets hurt we should not ____________. (bother/panic/eat)

3. Indicate whether the following statements are true (T) or false (F).

a. Crowd around an injured person. ☐

b. Wash the wound with clean water. ☐

c. An ice pack can be used on a burn. ☐

What safety rules will you follow in case of a fire?

 ISBN 978-81-8477-928-8

8
Solid, Liquid and Gas

We are surrounded by a number of things. These things have weight and occupy space. Any substance which has weight and occupies space is known as **matter**. Matter may be soft, hard, light or heavy.

Matter is made up of tiny particles known as **atoms**. These atoms are usually joined together in groups, known as **molecules**. A molecule is the smallest part of a substance that has all the characteristics of that substance.

States of Matter

Matter can exist in three states depending on how the molecules are packed or arranged. These states are solid, liquid and gas.

Solids are substances that have a fixed shape and a fixed size (**volume**). The molecules in solids are packed very tightly, that is, they are held together by strong bonds, so they don't move very easily.

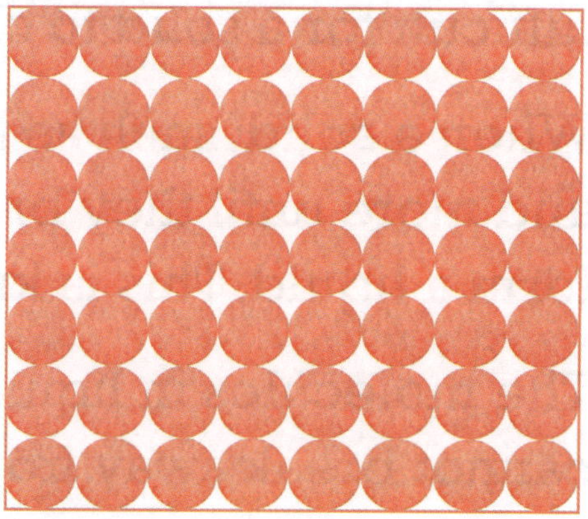

Hence, solids keep their shape and size. The shape of a solid does not change unless it is heated, cooled, broken or cut.

 ISBN 978-81-8477-928-8

Liquids are substances that do not have a fixed shape, but they have a fixed volume. They assume the shape of the container in which they are held. The molecules are not packed very tightly, that is, the molecules have weaker bonds. The molecules can move around slightly, so liquids can flow.

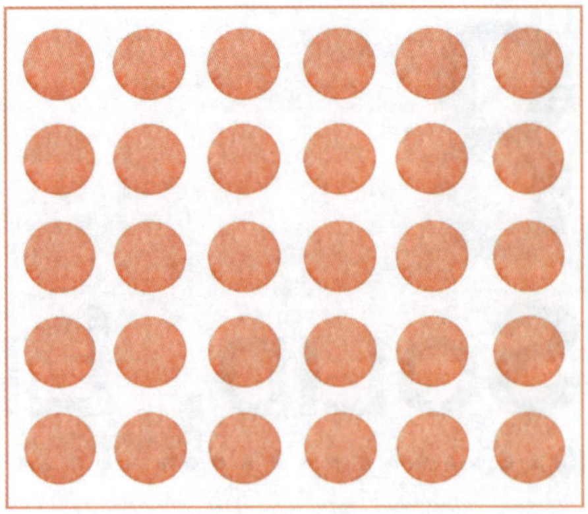

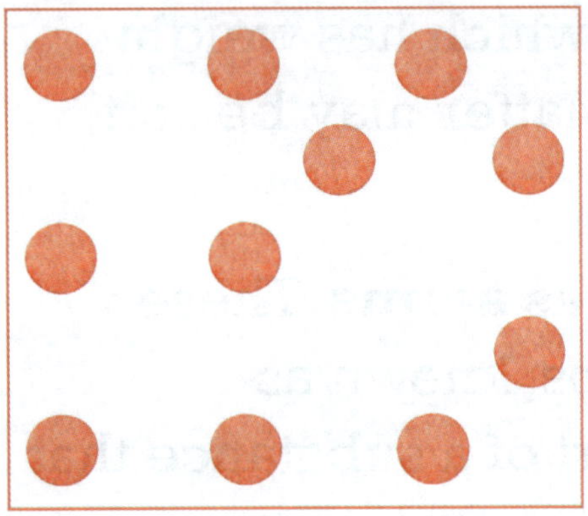

Gases are substances with very loosely packed matter. They do not have a fixed shape or a fixed volume. The molecules of gases are spread out in an open space freely. Gases cannot keep their shape unless kept in a sealed container. Most gases are colourless.

Changing the State of Matter

If the attraction between the molecules of a substance is strong, they are packed tightly together to make a solid. The particles in a solid are in a fixed position and this makes it difficult for a solid to change its shape.

When a solid, such as ice, is heated the particles vibrate more and more until they break away from each other. They then form a liquid. This is known as **melting**.

The molecules in liquids can move around quite freely, but cannot break away from each other completely. If we heat a liquid, the molecules move around very quickly. As the liquid becomes hotter, the molecules escape so quickly that the

 ISBN 978-81-8477-928-8

liquid begins to bubble. This is called **boiling.** Eventually, they move faster and faster and then escape from the surface of the liquid and become a gas. This is known as **evaporation**.

Circle Time

Bring in a bag of ice cubes. Make small groups or pairs with your classmates and find the fastest way to melt an ice cube. As you all know heat can change matter and adding more heat might make matter change faster. One group can put the ice cubes in a sunny spot, the second group can warm them up in their hands and the third group may just put them in a cup on their desks. How long does each method take? Which method was the best? Discuss with the rest of the class.

Physical and Chemical Changes

As we heat an ice cube, it changes into water. This is a **physical change** because the water in the ice cube changes its appearance. But it is easy to freeze the water back into ice again. In other words, the change is **reversible**. Liquid water can be heated to make steam. If the steam is cooled, it will turn back to liquid water. This is another reversible change.

However, if we heat a piece of paper, a different kind of change takes place. The paper first turns brown and becomes brittle. Then it bursts into flames and gives out a lot of heat. It finally becomes ash. When the ash has cooled down, it does not change back into paper. A completely new substance is

 ISBN 978-81-8477-928-8

formed. This type of change is **irreversible**. It is known as a **chemical change**.

Many changes that take place in nature are chemical changes. For example, when we cook food, the changes that take place are chemical changes.

Learn More

Find out why water pipes burst during winters in hilly regions.

Explore

Think about baking a cake. The batter is a liquid mixture of flour, sugar, water and other ingredients. When it is cooked in the oven, the batter turns into a delicious new 'solid'. It cannot be changed back into flour, sugar, water and other ingredients. The batter has undergone a chemical change that is irreversible and it has become something new.

mixing ingredients to bake a cake

Solubility is the ability of a substance to dissolve. In the process of dissolving, the substance which is being dissolved is called a **solute** and the substance in which the solute is dissolved is called the **solvent**. A mixture of a solute and a solvent is called a **solution**. When we mix sugar in water, sugar is the solute and water is the solvent.

 ISBN 978-81-8477-928-8

Quiz Time

1. Answer the questions.

a. What is matter?

b. Write three differences between solids, liquids and gases.

c. What is solubility? Give an example, clearly mentioning the solute and the solvent.

d. Give an example of a reversible change.

e. Name a material that can exist in all three states of matter.

f. Give an example where a liquid changes into a solid when it is cooled.

g. Give an example of a solid turning back into a liquid when it is heated.

h. What is a physical change?

i. What is a chemical change?

j. If you melt wax, is that a physical or chemical change? Explain.

2. Fill in the blanks to complete the sentences.

a. When a liquid changes into a gas, it is called ______________.

b. During a ______________ change, the product formed is completely new.

c. ______________ have a fixed shape.

d. Matter is made up of tiny particles called ______________.

e. ______________, ______________ and ______________ are the three states of matter.

 ISBN 978-81-8477-928-8

3. Define these and give three examples of each.

a. Solids

b. Liquids

c. Gases

4. Indicate whether the following statements are true (T) or false (F).

a. Some solids can be poured into a container. ☐

b. Liquids can be held easily in our hands. ☐

c. Liquids take the shape of the container they are poured into. ☐

d. If a liquid is poured from a small container to a big one, its volume will also increase. ☐

e. We can melt a substance by cooling it. ☐

f. Sand does not dissolve in water. ☐

g. In order to turn water into ice, we must heat up the liquid. ☐

h. The molecules in a solid are in a fixed position. ☐

i. When a solid is turned into a liquid by heat, it is called evaporation. ☐

j. Gases do not have a fixed volume or shape. ☐

 ISBN 978-81-8477-928-8

5. Mark the following as solid (S), liquid (L) or gas (G).

stone 	wood 
iron 	tea 
ice 	oil 
water 	juice 
lava 	gas balloon 
milk 	cola 

6. Write a short note.

a. Melting

b. Boiling

c. Evaporation

Why do clothes dry faster on a sunny day than on a cloudy day?

 ISBN 978-81-8477-928-8

9
FORCE, WORK AND ENERGY

In everyday life we pull, push, twist or turn a number of objects. Objects can be moved or their shape changed by the use of force.

FORCE

An object that is not moving will stay at rest unless force is applied to it. For example, a tennis ball will not move unless it is pushed, bounced or thrown. Once a body is moving, it requires a force to stop it. This tendency of a body to stay at rest, or to keep moving, is known as **inertia**. Force is required to overcome the inertia of a body and to make it change its state of being still or being in motion.

 ISBN 978-81-8477-928-8

It is easy to move an empty trolley and to stop it. However, when we place heavy packages in the same trolley, it becomes difficult to get it to start moving or stop it once it starts moving. In other words, as mass increases, greater force is required to get an object to move or to stop an object already in motion.

Types of Forces

There are many kinds of forces. Two of the most common types of forces we experience in our everyday life are—friction and gravity.

Friction

Rub your finger over a rough surface. You will notice that there appears to be a force trying to stop your finger from moving. This force is called friction. Friction is a force between two surfaces in contact, or trying to slide across one another.

friction prevents us from slipping and falling

Friction tends to stop two surfaces that are moving over each other easily. Rough surfaces offer greater friction than smoother ones. If there is no friction between the ground and the soles of our shoes, we would not be able to walk—we would keep slipping and falling.

Friction always works in the direction opposite to the direction of motion. It always slows down a moving object.

 ISBN 978-81-8477-928-8

Learn More

Encourage the students to think and answer.

- Which creates more friction—a skater on an ice skating rink or a piece of sandpaper rubbing against a piece of wood?
- How does a car stop when we apply brakes? Why do the tyres of cars skid more on wet roads than on dry roads?

Explore

Objective: To observe movements that cause friction.

Method: Try moving a pile of books on a carpet, a wooden table and a plastic countertop. Explain which surface created the greatest friction and explain why this is so.

Observation:

1. carpet ____________________
2. wood ____________________
3. plastic ____________________

Conclusion: ____________________

When we rub our hands together, the friction between our hands produces heat.

When we strike a match, the rubbing of the match on the rough surface creates enough heat to set fire to the chemicals at the end of the match.

rubbing our hands together produces heat

 ISBN 978-81-8477-928-8

As a spacecraft re-enters the Earth's atmosphere, there is a lot of friction between the air and the surface of the spacecraft. This produces a great deal of heat. To overcome this intense heat, shields are fitted around the spacecraft to protect the astronauts.

sliding down snow produces friction

In motor cars, oil is used to lessen the friction between the different metal parts. The oil forms a film between the metal surfaces, so that they do not rub against each other. This prevents the motor from overheating, and reduces the wear and tear on the parts.

Circle Time

There is less friction when we use rollers to move things rather than when we slide them. Slide a book and a marble across a table.

Observation: ______________________________

Conclusion: ______________________________

Gravity

When we hold a pencil and then drop it, it falls to the ground. For the pencil to fall downwards there has to be a force pulling it towards the ground. We can feel this force when we hold the object in our hand. This is known as **weight**.

 ISBN 978-81-8477-928-8

Sir Isaac Newton, an English scientist, was the first person to discover why things have weight and fall to the ground. It is said that after seeing an apple fall from a tree, he began thinking about why this should happen. His explanation was that the Earth and the apple attract each other. The Earth, being so large, is not affected by the pull of the apple. However, the apple, being smaller, is pulled towards the Earth.

The force attracting these things through space is known as gravity. Gravity is a force of attraction that acts between all objects. It is this force that holds everything to the Earth's surface and causes them to have weight. If there had been no gravity, all of us would have been floating in space.

The further we move away from the Earth, the pull of gravity reduces.

The total amount of matter in anything is known as its **mass**. The more mass something has, the more it is pulled towards the Earth by gravity and, therefore, the greater is its weight.

Factastic

Since the force of gravity on the Moon is one-sixth of the force of gravity on Earth, your weight on the Moon will be one-sixth of your weight on Earth. But your mass will be the same on the Earth and on the Moon.

Explore

Imagine you live on a planet that has no gravity. Explain how life would be on such a planet.

 ISBN 978-81-8477-928-8

Work and Machines

When an object is moved from its position by applying force, then work is said to be done. A machine is a device that makes work easier for us. It overcomes a force at one place by enabling a force to be applied somewhere else.

Machines are usually simple or complex. Complex machines usually contain versions or combinations of simple machines.

There are five simple machines.

- Ramp
- Pulley
- Lever
- Screw
- Wheel and axle

A **ramp** is an inclined plane that makes it easy to go up a short distance.

A **pulley** is a machine consisting of a wheel, which is designed to have a rope passing around it. A pulley enables us to lift heavy weights by pulling the rope downwards. It is much easier to lift something heavy, such as a car engine, by pulling it downwards, because of the force of gravity.

 ISBN 978-81-8477-928-8

A claw hammer, used to pull out nails, is an example of a **lever**. The point of balance of a lever, around which the lever works, is known as the fulcrum.

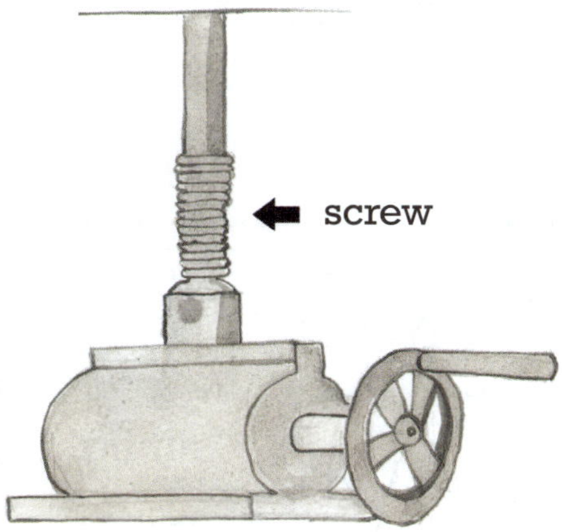

A **screw** is an inclined plane wrapped around a pole, which holds things together or lifts materials. Some common examples include wood and metal screws and the screws on jars and bottles and their tops.

The **wheel and axle** makes it possible to move heavy loads easily, as rolling friction is less than sliding friction.

ENERGY

Energy means the capacity to do work. For example, we can use the muscles in our arms to lift things. Our arms contain energy, which is used when the muscles work. When we cook food on the stove, energy from the fuel is used.

FORMS OF ENERGY

There are many forms of energy such as light energy, electrical energy and sound energy. All forms of energy are either potential or kinetic.

 ISBN 978-81-8477-928-8

Potential energy is stored in a stationary object. **Kinetic energy** is the energy within a moving object. Things at rest have potential energy, but once they begin to move, the energy becomes kinetic. For example, a parked car has potential energy. When it is driven, the car gains kinetic energy as it moves. Potential energy can be changed into kinetic energy and back again into potential energy.

Energy is captured in different forms.

Solar energy

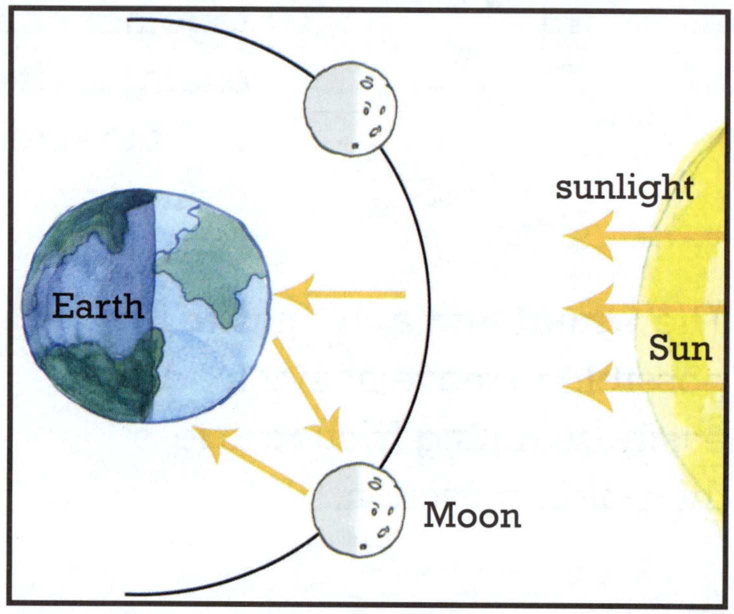

The Sun's energy reaches us in the form of heat and light. The source of light from the Sun, a star and a light bulb is known as **direct light**. When direct light from one object gets bounced off another object, it is called **reflected light**.

Moonlight is an example of reflected light. The direct light from the Sun reflects off the Moon to produce moonlight.

The energy that we receive from the Sun is known as **solar energy**.

Explore

Discuss the advantages of using solar energy over conventional forms of energy.

 ISBN 978-81-8477-928-8

Learn More

Use an encyclopedia to find out the different uses of solar energy. Create a chart to be displayed in the class.

Chemical energy

Chemical energy is stored in the particles that make up food and fuels. The food we eat gives chemical energy which allows us to move. When fuels, such as petrol and gas, are burned, they provide energy in the form of heat.

Sound energy

Sound is another form of energy that is transferred from a vibrating object and carried through the air to our ears. We can make sounds by making things vibrate. **Vibration** means shaking up and down or backwards and forwards very fast. There are different kinds of sounds. They can be high or low. High sounds are made by fast vibrations and low sounds are made by slow vibrations. Whether a sound is high or low or average is called the **pitch** of the sound. Most sounds we hear travel through the air.

Wind energy

The air that moves is known as wind. Wind can take the form of a gentle breeze or a destructive gale. We can use wind to transport us from place to place, for example, by using hang gliders or yachts. We also use wind energy to turn windmills to pump water and to generate electricity.

 ISBN 978-81-8477-928-8

Circle Time

Find out where in India are wind farms located. How much energy do they produce annually?

Electrical energy

Electrical energy can come from batteries and power plants. Power plants burn fuel to make electricity for homes and factories. Fans, computers, machines, refrigerators and other machines use electrical energy.

Hydro energy

Water has force. Moving water has a lot of energy. This energy is harvested by building dams on rivers. Dams allow the water to fall from a great height and with great force onto turbines creating energy. This energy from the water is used to generate electricity.

Explore

Objective: To understand the force of water.

Materials required: A piece of wood, a brick and a bucket of water.

Method: Gently lower a piece of wood into a bucket of water and then a brick and observe what happens to the wood.

Observation: ______________________________

Conclusion: ______________________________

ISBN 978-81-8477-928-8

Quiz Time

1. Answer the questions.

a. What is inertia?

b. What is meant by energy?

c. What is meant by kinetic energy?

d. What is friction? Give an example of how friction helps us.

e. What is used in cars to protect the moving parts? Why?

f. What is a pulley and what can it be used for?

g. What kind of machine is a wheel barrow an example of?

h. What is the name given to the energy stored in food or petrol?

i. What kind of vibration causes low sounds?

j. Which are the two most common types of force we experience in our daily life?

k. Write a few sentences about alternative sources of energy.

2. Fill in the blanks with the correct words from the brackets.

a. The energy present in moving things is called ____________ energy. (potential/solar/kinetic)

b. A ____________ is an inclined plane wrapped around a pole.(lever/screw/fulcrum)

c. ____________ energy is stored in food. (Physical/Solar/Chemical)

d. ____________ is an example of a simple machine. (Pulley/Gravity/Friction)

e. When we rub our hands together, ____________ is produced. (wind/heat/gravity)

 ISBN 978-81-8477-928-8

f. A see-saw is a kind of __________. (lever/fork/wheel)

g. A __________ helps us lift things. (screw/pulley/wheel)

h. We can use ______________ to help us join things. (wheels/screws/levers)

3. List three things that get their energy from

a. Electricity

b. Wind

c. Sunlight

4. Draw three examples of simple machines in your home. Choose one and describe how it is used.

5. Draw two musical instruments that make sounds using strings.

6. Look at the pictures. Draw the missing objects.

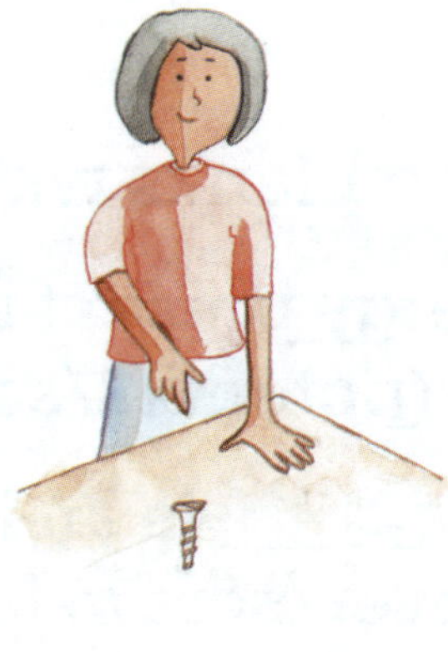

7. Indicate whether the following statements are true (T) or false (F).

a. A force is needed to make a stationary object move. ☐

b. A larger object falls to the ground more quickly than a smaller object. ☐

 ISBN 978-81-8477-928-8

c. Pushing and pulling are known as forces. ☐

d. As we go further away from the Earth, gravity gets stronger. ☐

e. The pull of gravity on the Moon is weaker than the pull of gravity on Earth. ☐

f. Mass is the name given to the total amount of matter in an object. ☐

8. Draw three pictures of ways in which we can utilise the force of the wind.

9. Squashing, bending, twisting and stretching can change the shape of objects. Will these things change (C), not change (NC) or bounce back (BB)? Write the correct answer in the boxes.

materials	squashing	bending	twisting	stretching
bag of sand				
sponge				
cotton reel				
elastic band				

Why is it difficult to open an umbrella on a windy day?

 ISBN 978-81-8477-928-8

10
Air and Weather

Atmosphere is the blanket of air that surrounds the Earth. It is made up of gases, water vapour and impurities such as dust and smoke.

Layers of the Atmosphere

The atmosphere consists of five layers that are held together by the gravitational force. It helps to keep the Earth's warmth from escaping into space at night. If the atmosphere was not present, the temperature during the day would be more than 110°C, and at night it would be a freezing -145°C. The atmosphere protects us from meteors as well. Due to the friction generated between a meteor and the atmosphere, most meteors burn up before hitting the Earth's surface.

The **troposphere** is the lowest layer, where we live and which contains 90% of the air in the atmosphere. It extends up to a height of 7 to 20 kms above sea level. Air is the warmest near ground level of the troposphere. The higher we go the colder it gets.

The **stratosphere** is the second layer of the Earth's atmosphere extending to a height of about 50 kms from sea level. It contains a layer of **ozone** that protects us from the harmful effects of the Sun's ultraviolet rays. The lower stratosphere has (nearly)

 ISBN 978-81-8477-928-8

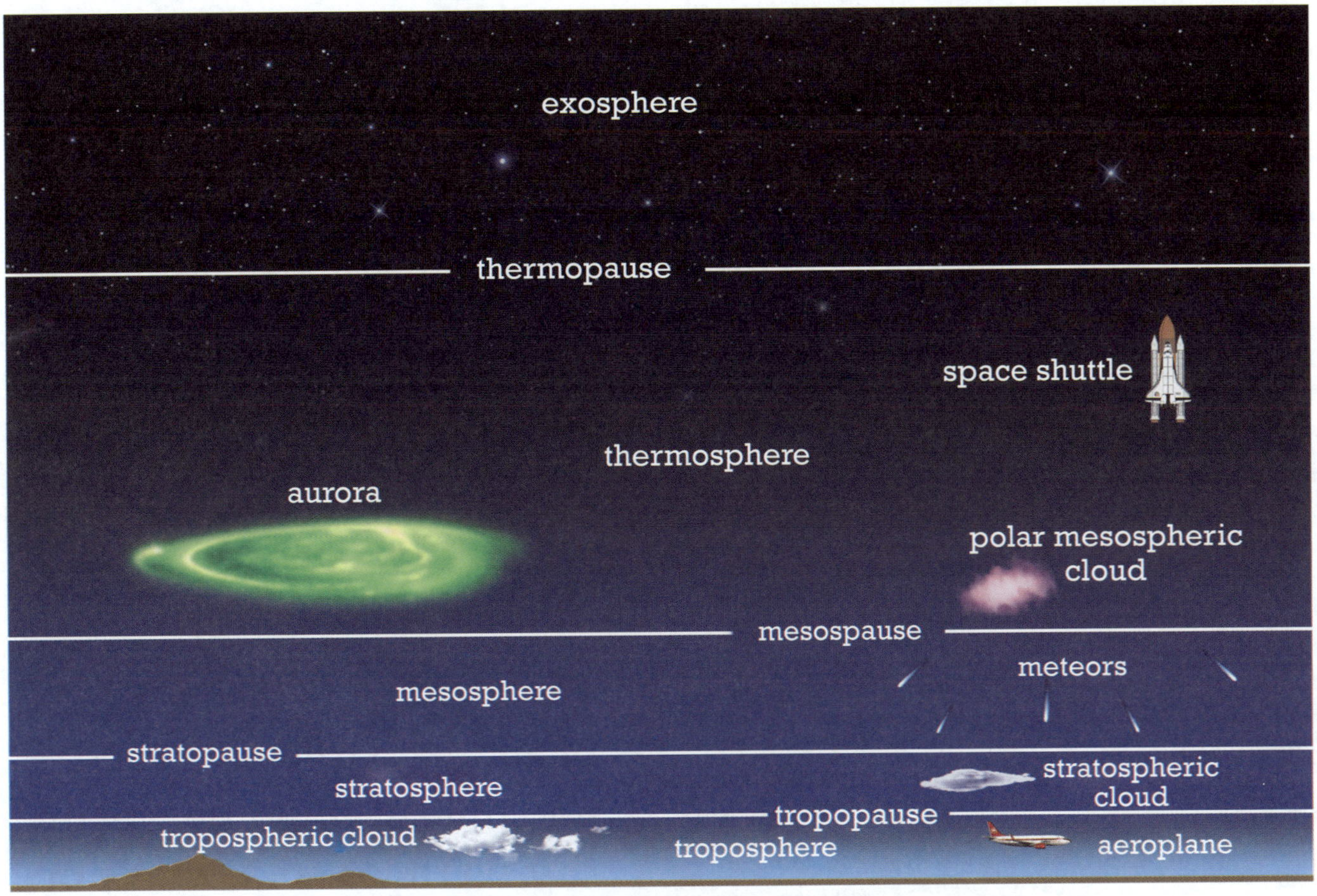

different layers of the atmosphere

constant temperature while the temperature rises with the increase in altitude due to the absorption of sunlight by ozone.

The **mesosphere** is the third layer extending between 50 to 80 kms above sea level. It is the coldest layer of the atmosphere with temperatures dipping to as low as -100°C. Meteors burn up in this layer as they enter the Earth's atmosphere.

The **thermosphere** extends from 90 to between 500 and 1000 kms above sea level. Space shuttles fly in this region. Temperatures in the higher region of the thermosphere range between 500°C to 2,000°C.

The **exosphere** is the fifth and the outermost layer of the atmosphere where several satellites orbit the Earth. With this layer, the atmosphere merges with space.

 ISBN 978-81-8477-928-8

Circle Time

The ozone layer absorbs harmful ultraviolet radiation, which protects us from skin cancer. Ozone depletion has been a cause for concern, particularly in the Southern Hemisphere. Discuss ways in which you can contribute to protecting the ozone layer.

WEATHER

Movements within the atmosphere give rise to weather conditions and provide a source of energy in the form of wind energy.

> **Factastic**
> Modern planes fly at very high altitudes where there is very little oxygen. Pressurised air cabins on flights ensure that passengers and crew have enough oxygen and are able to breathe comfortably.

The weather is the state of air at a particular place and time. It could be wet or dry, warm or cold, windy or cloudy.

When a normal pattern of weather in a particular area extends over a long period of time, it is known as the **climate** of that place. The climate of a particular country tells us how hot, cold or wet it will be at that place at different times of the year.

The higher we go above the sea level, the thinner the air in the atmosphere becomes. On very high mountains, the air is too thin to breathe in comfort.

Although we cannot see air, we feel it only when it moves as **wind** or as a **breeze**. A strong wind is known as a **gale** and very strong winds are known as **storms**.

Storms that are accompanied by thunder as well as lightning are known as **thunderstorms**.

 ISBN 978-81-8477-928-8

Wind affects the weather of a place. It exerts pressure that helps birds, aeroplanes and kites to fly in the air.

In coastal areas, the direction of the wind changes depending on the time of the day or night. During the day, land becomes hotter than water. The hot air rises up from land and is displaced by the cool breeze from the sea. These **sea breezes** cool the land. During the night, land cools down faster than the sea. As the hot air over the sea rises, this is displaced by the cool breeze from the land. These are known as **land breezes**.

The Sun plays a very important role in changing the weather conditions on Earth. The Earth is slightly tilted on its axis as it revolves around the Sun, such that the side of the Earth which is closer to the Sun always gets longer, hotter days. This part of the Earth experiences summer. The part of Earth, which is away from the Sun experiences cooler, shorter days of winter.

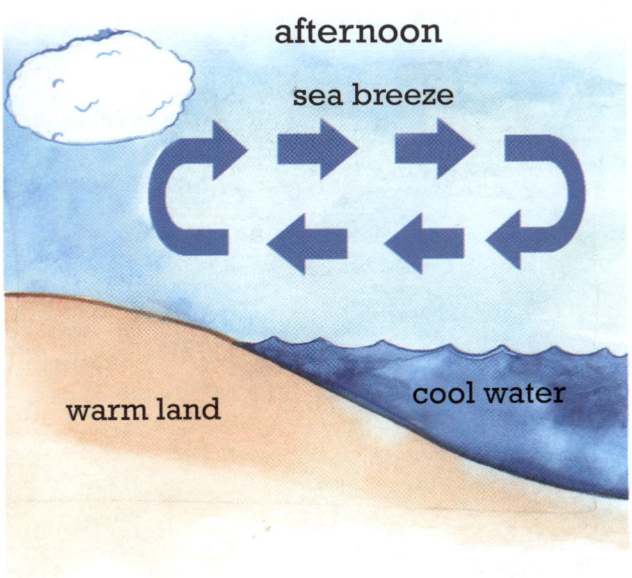

sea breeze

land breeze

 ISBN 978-81-8477-928-8

Therefore, the rotation of the Earth on its axis causes day and night, and the revolution of the Earth around the Sun causes seasons—spring, summer, monsoon, autumn and winter.

The Sun also causes changes in the waterbodies on Earth. The amount of water vapour in the air is known as the **humidity** in the air. Heat from the Sun's rays changes water into water vapour. Water vapour condenses to form tiny droplets of water suspended in the air. These droplets combine together to form clouds.

Clouds are masses of airborne water droplets.

water cycle

rotation: to turn all the way around or spins on an axis
revolution: to travel around an object

  ISBN 978-81-8477-928-8

The rain we see has fallen millions of times before. The Sun heats the oceans, rivers and lakes, and countless litres of water rise into air as invisible water vapour, through the process known as **evaporation**.

The liquid evaporates or dries up and hence puddles and clothes become dry. Evaporation happens when a liquid turns into gas.

Quiz Time

1. Answer the questions.

a. Write a few sentences about land breezes.

b. Why do clothes take longer to dry on a rainy day?

c. Why does coastal Gujarat have cooler summers than Rajasthan?

d. How does wind affect the weather of a place?

e. If the atmosphere did not exist, what conditions would exist on Earth?

f. Describe how the Sun affects the seasons on the Earth.

g. Describe the ways in which water returns to the Earth.

h. Describe how the water cycle works. Illustrate your answer with a diagram.

i. What happens to water vapour when it cools down?

 ISBN 978-81-8477-928-8

2. Fill in the blanks to complete the sentences.

a. _______________ is the layer of the atmosphere we live in.

b. The higher we go, the _______________ the air in the atmosphere becomes.

c. _______________ are masses of airborne water droplets.

d. A strong wind is known as a _______________.

e. Water rises from the oceans to the air due to _______________.

3. Complete the water cycle using the words given in the box.

Sun	sea	rain	groundwater
clouds	sea	sky	vapour

E_AP_ _AT_ _N—The _______________ shines and water is drawn up from the _______________ to the _______________ to form water _______________.

C_ _DEN_AT_ _N—As the water vapour rises into the sky it cools and forms _______________. The water droplets become larger and it starts to _______________.

Some of the water sinks to the ground, which is called _______________. Some of it drains into streams and rivers and ends up back in the _______________.

 ISBN 978-81-8477-928-8

4. Mark the surfaces on which water vapour will condense in these rooms.

Does the weather each day remain the same during one entire season? Give examples with your answer.

 ISBN 978-81-8477-928-8

11
The Earth and the Solar System

The solar system comprises of the Sun and everything that travels around it. Our solar system is elliptical in shape with the Sun at its centre. Eight known planets and their moons, along with comets, asteroids, meteoroids and other space objects orbit the Sun and are in continuous motion.

The Sun is 150 million kms away from the Earth. It makes up about 99% of the total mass of the solar system.

The inner planets—Mercury, Venus, Earth and Mars—have similar compositions and are known as the **terrestrial planets**. They are small in size and are made up of rock and metals. The outer planets—Jupiter, Saturn, Uranus and Neptune—are known as the **gas giants**. They are very large in size and are composed of gases. Comets, asteroids, meteoroids, dust and gases are all part of the solar system. Meteoroids are small pieces of rock and asteroids are giant chunks of rock.

Sun

The Sun is a yellow dwarf star and is believed to be about 4 billion years old. It spins on its axis as it revolves around the **Milky Way**.

Factastic
Solar flares shoot fast-moving particles from the surface of the Sun. Some of these flares strike the atmosphere of the Earth creating a glow known as an aurora.

 ISBN 978-81-8477-928-8

The core of the Sun is extremely hot. Heat and light is generated by the Sun. The Sun also produces huge explosions of energy known as **solar flares**.

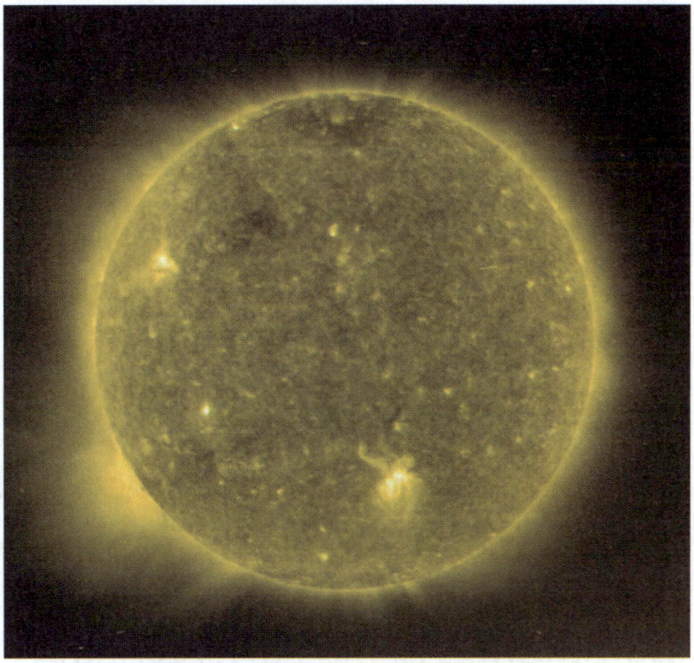

The Sun has a massive diameter of 13,93,000 km.

Circle Time

The word solar stems from the Roman word for the god of the Sun, Sol. Therefore, the word solar refers to the Sun and solar power is power from the Sun. When we say something is solar powered, it means that the energy is produced directly from sunlight.

Find out the different applications of solar power that is in use.

Stars

We can see billions of stars in the night sky. The sizes of the stars vary, some are small dwarf stars while others are super giants. New stars are being formed at all times. Stars appear to shine and twinkle as they burn up nuclear fuel. As this fuel is burned up, the star eventually dies out. When seen from the Earth, several groups of stars appear to form patterns. These groups of stars are called **constellations**.

 ISBN 978-81-8477-928-8

A **galaxy** is a system of millions or billions of stars, gases and dust, held together by gravitational attraction. The Sun and the solar system form part of the Milky Way galaxy, which is one of the many galaxies in the universe.

> **Factastic**
> Shooting stars are not stars, but meteors that flare up as they enter the Earth's atmosphere and burn up due to friction.

How brightly a star shines depends on the amount of energy it produces. The colour of a star depends on the temperature of the surface of the star. Blue stars are the hottest, followed by white stars. Yellow, orange and red stars are the coolest stars in decreasing order of their surface temperatures.

> **Factastic**
> Most stars exist in pairs that orbit each other. The Sun is a single star, but this is uncommon.

Earth

The Earth obtains heat and light as solar energy from the Sun. The Sun plays a very important role in the water cycle and thus the existence of the Earth. It causes the evaporation of water from the Earth's surface which in turn leads to rainfall or snow.

The outside of the Earth is known as its surface, which is part land and part water. Water covers more than two-thirds of the Earth's surface.

The Earth can be divided into

- the biosphere, which includes all forms of life, both on land and on sea.
- the hydrosphere, which includes surface water on Earth.
- the internal structure of the Earth, which includes the crust, the mantle and the core of the Earth.

 ISBN 978-81-8477-928-8

The land on the surface of the Earth is not the same everywhere. It has high mountains, plains, dry deserts, tropical rainforests and ice covered areas.

> **Factastic**
> It was once believed that the Earth was at the centre of the solar system. But a Polish astronomer named Nicolaus Copernicus (1473–1543) was the first to put forward the theory that the planets, including the Earth, revolve around the Sun.

Most parts of land are covered in soil. The depth of soil varies from only a few centimetres to many metres. Plants, which sustain all animal life forms, grow in this soil.

The parts of the Earth covered with water also vary. There are oceans, seas, rivers, lakes and ponds. Some are very large and deep, while others are small and shallow.

The Earth is divided into regions known as **hemispheres**. The **equator** is an imaginary line that divides the Earth into the Northern Hemisphere and the Southern Hemisphere. The length of the equator is about 40,075 km.

> **Factastic**
> The Earth's atmosphere comprises one millionth the total mass of the Earth. It contains 21% oxygen, 78% nitrogen and 0.9% argon. In addition, it contains water vapour, carbon dioxide, neon, methane, krypton, helium, hydrogen, carbon monoxide, ozone and other gases. The Earth's atmosphere is responsible for making life possible on it.

The Earth goes around the Sun, completing one revolution in 365 and a quarter days or in one complete year. As the Earth orbits around the Sun, it also spins on its own axis, which is tipped at an angle of 23.5°. It takes one day or twenty-four hours to complete one rotation on its axis.

 ISBN 978-81-8477-928-8

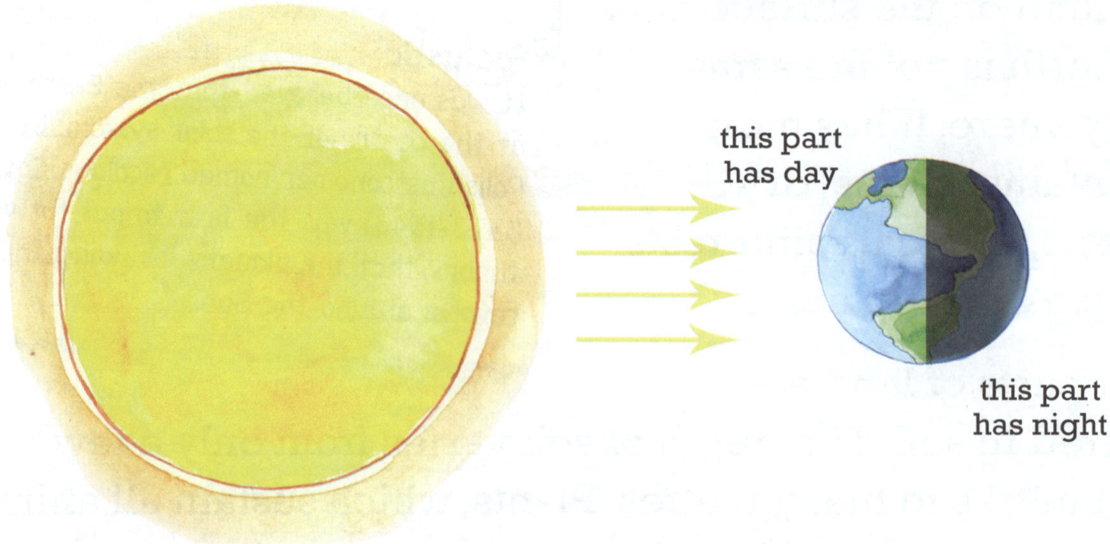

At any time, half of the Earth faces the Sun and therefore receives light

Seasons

The tilt in the Earth's axis is responsible for the seasons and the different temperatures throughout the year.

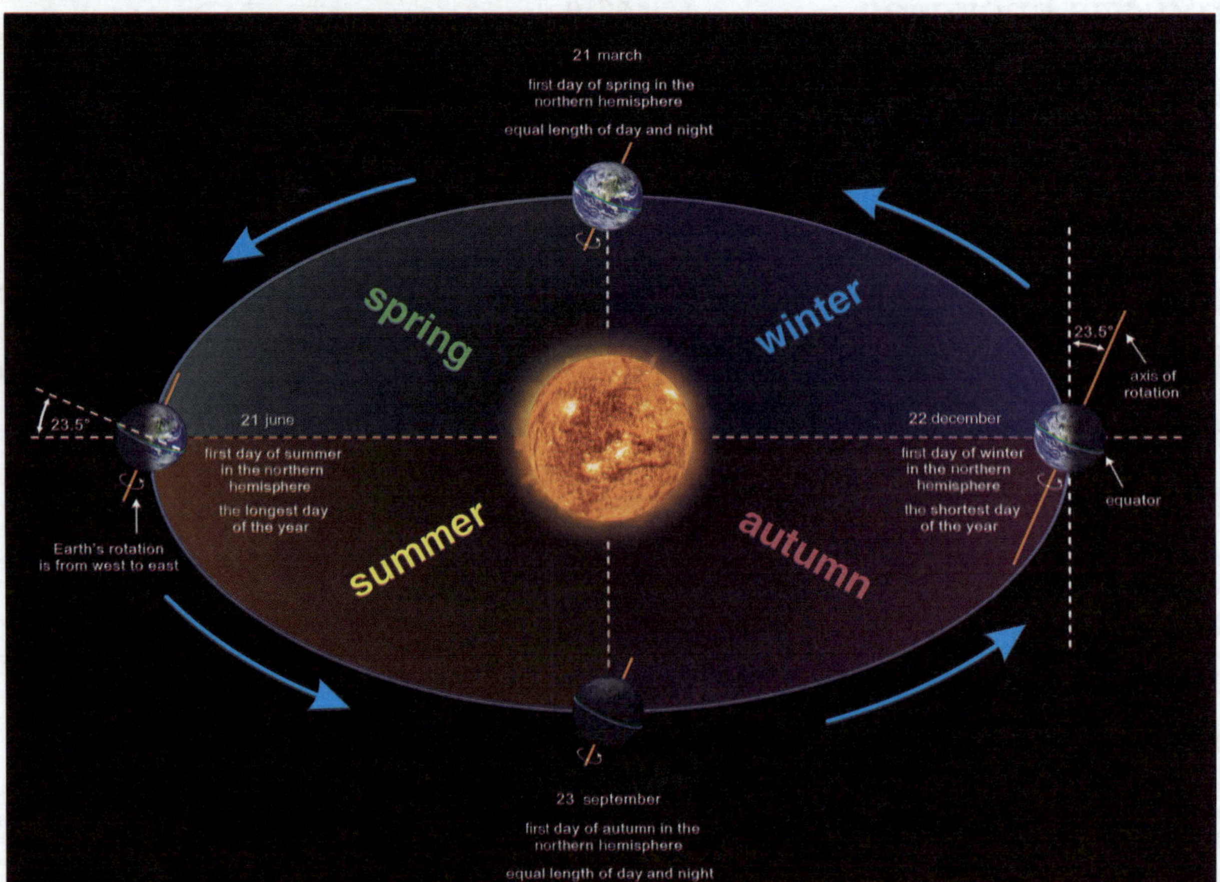

 ISBN 978-81-8477-928-8

The Sun shines more directly on the Earth's Northern Hemisphere in June, and more directly on the Southern Hemisphere in December.

In spring and autumn, the Sun shines fairly straight down on the equator, giving both hemispheres equal heat.

Explore

Objective: To understand the different seasons on Earth.

Method: Take a globe and a light bulb or flashlight. Imagine the globe is the Earth and the light is the Sun.

Observation: ____________________________________

____

____

Moon

The Moon orbits the Earth, just as the Earth orbits the Sun.

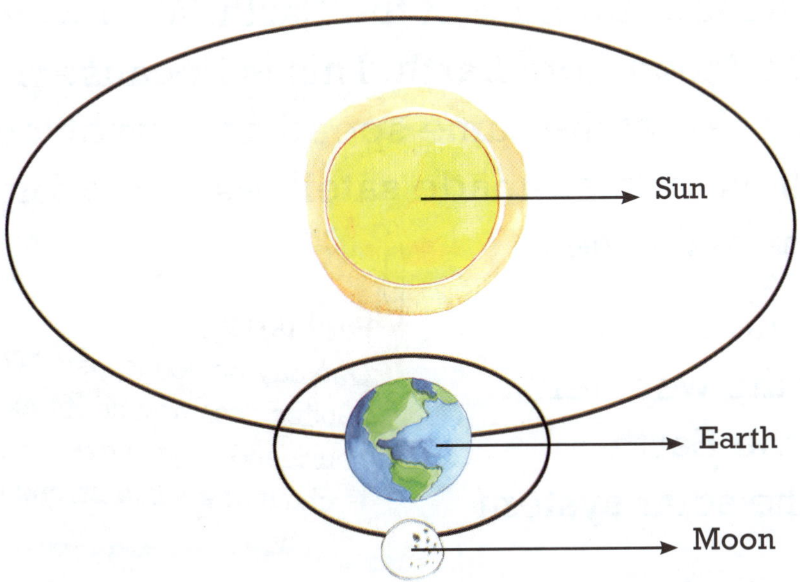

 ISBN 978-81-8477-928-8

> **Factastic**
> On 20 July 1969, astronauts Neil Armstrong and Edwin Aldrin landed the Lunar Module of *Apollo 11* on the Moon's surface.

The surface of the Moon is made up of plains, mountains, valleys and craters. There is no air on the Moon. It does not have an atmosphere to protect it from the extreme heat and cold. The temperature of the surface of the Moon can be more than 100°C and as low as -173°C.

The Moon travels around the Earth in an oval orbit. It orbits the Earth once every twenty-nine days. Although the Moon is much smaller than the Earth, its gravitational pull affects the Earth's ocean tides. The force of gravity on the Moon's surface is one-sixth of that on Earth.

Learn More

Make craters by throwing objects into dirt, flour or play dough.

The Moon is a natural satellite of the Earth. We always see the same side of the Moon from Earth. This is because the Moon rotates about its axis at the same speed as it revolves around the Earth. Artificial or man-made satellites also orbit the Earth. These have four main uses.

- Communication
- Monitoring the weather
- Observing the Earth
- Exploring the solar system

> **Factastic**
> One day on Venus lasts 117 Earth days. Jupiter goes around its axis in just 9 hours and 57 minutes. One day on Mars is about the same as one day on Earth.

 ISBN 978-81-8477-928-8

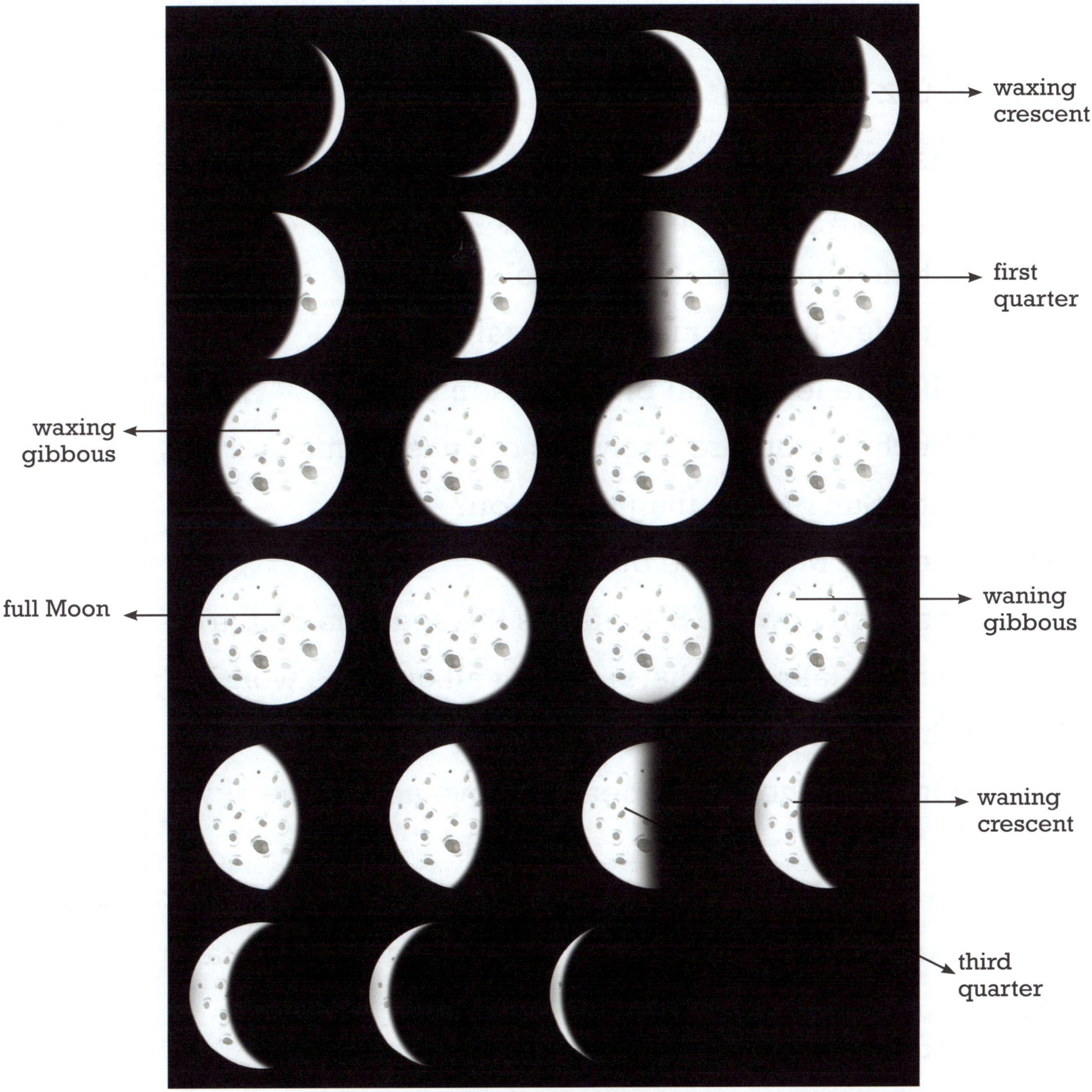

Phases of the Moon

Learn More

Find out the names of some Indian satellites in space.

 ISBN 978-81-8477-928-8

Quiz Time

1. Answer the questions.

a. What is a galaxy? Name a few.

b. List the components of the solar system.

c. List a few uses of man-made satellites.

d. What are terrestrial planets? Name them.

e. Which planets are known as the gas giants and why?

f. Is the Sun bigger than the Moon?

g. Does the Moon give out light?

h. Describe how the Sun affects the seasons on Earth.

i. As night falls in India, is it night all over the world? Explain.

j. Why does the Sun seem to disappear at night?

k. Why does the Sun appear to move across the sky?

2. Fill in the blanks with the correct words from the brackets.

a. The Moon orbits the ___________. (Earth/Sun/stars)

b. Groups of stars are called ___________.
(Milky Way/constellations/galaxy)

c. The Earth orbits the ___________. (Moon/Sun/Venus)

d. The ___________ is a natural satellite of the Earth.
(Sun/Mercury/Moon)

e. It takes twenty-four hours to complete one ___________.
(rotation/revolution/orbit)

ISBN 978-81-8477-928-8

3. Fill in the blanks to complete the sentences.

The Earth spins on its axis every __________ hours. Because of this spin, the Sun appears to rise in the __________ and set in the __________. While the Earth is spinning, the side that faces the Sun has __________.

4. Match the words with the correct definitions.

a.	axis	the force that pulls matter towards the centre of the Earth
b.	gravity	when it appears that the Sun is going down in the west
c.	sunset	an imaginary line running through the poles of the Earth
d.	orbit	when it appears that the Sun has risen in the east
e.	sunrise	the path an object takes around another object in space
f.	solar system	a shape like a ball
g.	sphere	the system of planets, along with the Sun, around which they revolve

Do you know the shape of the Earth? Support your answer with examples.

ISBN 978-81-8477-928-8

12 TAKING CARE OF OUR EARTH

The Earth is a wonderful place which we share with plants, animals and birds.

POLLUTION

Pollution is the introduction of harmful substances or products into the environment. A **pollutant** is any substance that contaminates air, water and land. As these harmful substances, gases, chemicals and garbage are added to the environment, they affect the quality of life of all living beings. Pollution is very dangerous for our health and environment. It can cause sickness and death in living beings, unnatural weather conditions and damage to crops.

There are different kinds of pollution, the most common being air, water, soil and noise pollution.

Some easy ways to take care of the Earth are

- Use electricity and petrol judiciously. Switch to using CNG (compressed natural gas) as a fuel for motor vehicles.

 ISBN 978-81-8477-928-8

- Discourage people from smoking in public places.
- Plant more trees all around to enrich the environment.
- Walk, cycle or use public transportation whenever possible.
- Turn off the lights, TV, radio and other electrical items when not in use.
- Don't pour chemicals down the storm sewer.
- Fix taps, faucets and pipes that are leaking to save water.
- Use safer alternatives to pesticides.
- Reduce, reuse, recycle.
- Keep the volume of music and the television down at home so that you don't disturb the other family members or your neighbours.

Air Pollution

All living beings rely on clean air to survive. Air pollution is the addition of substances to the atmosphere that can cause danger to human health and to other living matter that breathe this polluted air. The burning of fossil fuels (coal and oil) to generate heat and power for human consumption is the main source of air pollution. Transportation and burning of industrial wastes and other solid wastes also cause air pollution. Air has no colour or smell, except when it is polluted.

I Care...

We must preserve the land we live on.

 ISBN 978-81-8477-928-8

Explore

Find out the main types of pollutants that cause air pollution.

Bits of dust, metal, soot, gases and other materials are released from construction sites, factories and cars. These small particles reduce the quality of the air that we breathe causing respiratory diseases such as lung cancer, asthma and bronchitis.

Water Pollution

Plants and animals need fresh water to survive. The addition of harmful substances, such as oil and other wastes, to waterbodies, such as lakes, rivers, oceans and groundwater, contaminate or pollute the water, making it toxic. This causes diseases such as cholera, jaundice and diarrhoea. Stagnant water becomes a breeding place for mosquitoes. Mosquitoes spread diseases such as malaria, filaria and dengue.

Examples of water pollution.

- The water that we use for household chores, such as washing, bathing and cleaning, usually goes to sewage treatment plants to be purified. This water is treated to remove dirt, food waste and a number of other pollutants from it before it reaches the rivers. Most detergents and other chemical cleaning agents remain in the water and pass through the treatment plant untreated.
- Dirt and litter from the streets are washed into storm drains. This uncleaned and untreated water reaches the rivers, lakes and sea.

 ISBN 978-81-8477-928-8

- The oil that spills from tankers and ships causes destruction to marine life, as it pollutes the water and makes it poisonous for creatures and plants living in and off our seas and oceans..

Explore

Use the Internet to find out about hazardous wastes.

Soil Pollution

Soil is used for a variety of purposes.

When humans overuse or exploit soil, it gets polluted. There are many reasons for soil pollution.

- Overuse of fertilisers, pesticides and insecticides by the farmers for growing crops, poisons the soil after a few years.
- Cutting trees and forest fires destroy the natural habitat of plants and animals.
- Dumping industrial and household wastes in the soil.
- Overgrazing by animals makes the soil loose and leads to soil erosion.
- Construction activities also cause soil pollution.

 ISBN 978-81-8477-928-8

Noise Pollution

Big towns and cities are crowded with cars, trucks, buses, machines, alarms and sirens. When vehicles, horns and machines make loud, blaring sounds they cause noise pollution. Some people living in noisy areas, such as near airports or railway stations, are exposed to noise pollution all day.

Exposure to these loud sounds over a long period of time may damage our hearing. Noise pollution can cause other serious health problems as well.

Circle Time

Design posters for your school and display them.

Explore

Make a list of ways in which the Earth is being polluted. Think of ways you can contribute and prevent pollution.

Effects of Pollution

When a plant or an animal species no longer exists on Earth, that species is said to be **extinct**.

Extinction can take place in a number of ways and for a number of reasons. It could happen when a species is dependent on a particular type of food, which becomes unavailable, or the Earth becomes too hot or too cold for its survival.

 ISBN 978-81-8477-928-8

Mass extinction occurs when many species of animals and plants become extinct at the same time. Scientists believe there have been ten or more mass extinctions over the last 600 million years. These may have been due to gradual changes in climate over millions of years, or by the Earth being periodically hit by comet showers, leaving dust clouds that shut out the light from the Sun.

Today there are many thousands of species of plants and animals that are in danger of becoming extinct. These are known as **endangered** species.

Pollution affects our health in many ways. Air pollution may cause asthma, heart and lung disease. Pollution has destroyed and polluted the habitats of many animals. We have hunted down three birds—the dodo, the passenger pigeon and the giant moa—to extinction.

Large mammals, such as elephants, rhinos and giraffes, are threatened today. This is because their habitats have been destroyed and they are hunted by poachers for their meat, skin, horns and tusks. Jaguars, snow leopards, tigers, bears and even members of the ape family are now extinct in many of the areas in which they once lived. Many of these creatures need a large territory in which to hunt and breed. Encroaching cities, towns and farms have made this impossible.

Frogs, reptiles and fish are endangered by the draining of wetlands, pollution of waterways, destruction of rainforests and also by smuggling.

Factastic

A plant or animal is considered extinct if over a period of fifty years, repeated searches find no living beings of that species. Before that stage, it is classified as rare or at risk.

 ISBN 978-81-8477-928-8

Conservation

Today most countries are working towards conserving or preserving their native flora and fauna. The setting up of marine parks, national parks, reserves and wilderness areas has helped to conserve many plants and animals that otherwise would have become extinct. For example, efforts are continuously being made to preserve tigers from extinction. Project Tiger is a wildlife conservation project, launched in 1972 to protect the diminishing population of the Indian tigers. Some countries have also introduced programmes in which rare species are bred in captivity and, as their numbers increase, they are released back into the wild.

Learn More

Make a chart about ways in which the four kinds of pollution can be cut down. Write down the changes that you need to make in your life to help cut down on pollution.

 ISBN 978-81-8477-928-8

Quiz Time

1. Answer the questions.

a. Define pollution.

b. What are the main sources of air pollution?

c. Give an example of water pollution from everyday life.

d. Give some reasons for soil pollution.

e. Explain what is meant by the term endangered species?

f. Apart from human interference, what else can cause animal extinction?

g. What is meant when it is said that a plant or an animal is extinct?

h. What is meant by conservation?

2. Fill in the blanks and complete the sentences.

a. CNG is ____________ ____________ ____________.

b. When a species no longer exists on the Earth, it is said to be ____________.

c. Reduce, ____________, ____________.

d. ____________ is a contaminated water-borne disease.

e. ____________ by animals leads to soil erosion.

 ISBN 978-81-8477-928-8

3. Project Work

Divide the class into three groups. Each group can take one of the following projects as a group activity, collect information and make a presentation.

a. How to Save Trees: Prevent Deforestation

b. Van Mahotsav

c. World Environment Day

Read about dinosaurs and find out reasons for their mass extinction.

 ISBN 978-81-8477-928-8

How to Make a Project

Science experiments and projects (and presentations) are a fantastic part of learning that allow one to engage in hands-on learning experiences. They enhance reasoning and analytical abilities as they feed the curiosity of the students.

1. **Title** – For a science project, choose a catchy title. The title could reflect on the contents of the project. It is crucial to state the essential purpose of the project.
2. **Introduction and Purpose** – This section introduces the topic of the project. It briefly explains any information already available and states the purpose of the project. State why you are interested in this topic and include citations (if any) in this section.
3. **The Hypothesis or Question** – Use this section to state your hypothesis or raise the questions that the project aims to address.
4. **Materials and Methods** – All the materials used in the project should be listed in this section. You may also describe the entire procedure used to perform the project.
5. **Data and Results** – Data refers to the actual numbers or other information obtained in the project. This information can be presented in tables or charts. The results section is where the data is used to reach the conclusion.
6. **Conclusion** – The focus of the conclusion should be to answer the question raised in the third section. Here the data and its results should be compared and its findings should be clearly mentioned.

Alternatively, you may use the format below while starting out with a new experiment or project.

project planning	tasks	approximate number of hours
Choose a subject.		
Research information on the Internet or at the library.		
Study the information/data collected.		
Make a plan for the topic selected.		
Collect material required. (Most of the material required can be procured from around the house. Others may be easily available in retail stores.)		
Set up and perform experiments.		
Record data.		
Analyse data.		
Write a summary.		
In case of a presentation: • shop for a poster board and display materials • print out final copies of your work • put together the board presentation		
TOTAL (Add up the total estimated hours.)		

 ISBN 978-81-8477-928-8

How to Use an Encyclopedia

An encyclopedia is a useful resource found in all libraries. An encyclopedia may be a single volume, subject specific, or multi volume covering a wide range of topics. Because encyclopedias are so easy to use and so accessible, many people use encyclopedias as their first option for a reference tool.

Most general encyclopedias are multivolume sets and are set up in alphabetical format. Some encyclopedias may need you to know the key word or subject heading in order to find specific information covered over a variety of volumes. Some encyclopedias devote separate volumes to different subjects.

Locate the index. The index is usually in the last series of volumes and is in alphabetical order. It gives you page numbers and volume numbers to locate the article you are researching.

Read the article and pick out relevant information for your project.

For teachers

A. Pass a volume of an encyclopedia to a group of students. Ask them to go through the layout, the way the information is organised and the quickest way to locate an entry. Challenge each group to compile an encyclopedia on any topic. Topics could be children's authors, unique inventions, historical sites in Asia, etc.

B. Ask the students to read an entry on any animal of their choice. Encourage the students to write a newspaper article or a poem using all the details and facts from the entry.

Pink is my nose

I thrive on garbage

Go away, my friend

Tips

- Look out for other cross-references that can broaden your topic and provide new insight into your research.
- Pay attention to the maps, graphs and pictures in the article.
- The outline, provided for longer articles, is a helpful reference tool when organising your writing.
- Refer to authors correctly. The information on authors is either in the introductory material or in the index.

 ISBN 978-81-8477-928-8

How to Use the Internet

One of the most recent and popular resource for research is the Internet. The Internet is a repository of information collected from various sources. Navigating through sites and links can give you updated information. Though the Internet is a wealth of information, before proceeding on any topic, take an adult's help to determine which sites might be reliable and which might not be a good source.

For teachers

Divide the class into four groups. Give three groups a topic to research and present. These groups will have different resources to research. The fourth group will then review the depth and breadth of the information, and survey and compare all the sources. They can present their report based on:

Which source gave you more information?

Which source gave you better information?

Tips

- It is a good idea to sit with an adult and bookmark the sites that you will need for research. This way you can directly go to the pages you want to view.
- Before beginning the topic, write down some keywords on which you will base your research.
- Use quality, child-friendly search engines such as www.ajkids.com (Ask Jeeves Kids) and www.yahooligans.com (Yahooligans!). You can keep a list of helpful sites near the computer for easy access.
- Quotation marks are important while conducting a topic search. If you enter your topic or key words without quotation marks around it, the search will give information about anything linked to the words. If you put the search topic in quotation marks, you will get information related to the exact words placed within quotation marks.
- If you can't read through the entire article, you can use the FIND option to locate a particular word in the article.

 ISBN 978-81-8477-928-8